Schizophrenic America

Forthcoming from
Skaeg Books

LETTERS TO MOM – AN ADOLESCENT ABROAD
by Peter and Marie Salten

THE POET ANDREW SKIGG
by Elbert Shamroc

Schizophrenic America

Anni Damgaard

Skaeg Books
PHOENIX

Copyright © 2016 by Anni Damgaard
   All rights reserved

ISBN: 978-1-945258-01-5
   978-1-945258-00-8 (pbk)
   978-1-945258-02-2 (epub)
   978-1-945258-03-9 (mobi)

Library of Congress Control Number: 2016938908

Cover photo Copyright © 2016 by STJ

SchizophrenicAmerica.org (schizoam.org)

SkaegBooks.com

Contact: publisher@skaegbooks.com

Skaeg Books is an imprint of Skaeg Publishing, LLC

Skaeg Books and the Skaeg logos are trademarks of
   Skaeg Publishing, LLC

Book design by STJ – 5p

skaeg (skāg) 1. beard; 2. enjoyable, informed, cool. [Dan skæg]

*To my students
whose questions and concerns
inspired this book*

Acknowledgments

First and foremost I want to thank STJ at Skaeg Books for his invaluable editorial assistance in writing *Schizophrenic America*. I appreciate his tireless effort and encouragement.

I also want to thank Diane, Jeanne H, and Jerry for reading drafts and providing informative feedback.

Lastly, I want to thank two of my "students of change" – Jay and Niko – who spent many hours discussing sociology with me. I learned much listening to their concerns and dreams. They give me hope that a new and prosperous America can evolve.

Contents

Preface – xi

Introduction – 3

Part I. Our Schizophrenic Malady: Its Origin and Nature – 13

    1. The Cultural *I-ME* Dialogue – 15

    2. The Derailed *I-ME* Dialogue – 23

    3. The Birth of Individualism – 33

    4. Protestantism and the Spirit of Capitalism – 41

    5. Fostering the Growth of Capitalism – 49

    6. Social Darwinism – 55

    7. The Aesthetic Stage – 65

    8. History Repeats Itself – 69

    9. Sacred versus Secular Life – 77

Part II. A Holistic Reorientation to Life and Living – 85

    10. Reframing Our Protestant Ethos – 87

    11. Revolutionizing Our Cultural Mosaic – 95

    12. *I People* and *Me People* – 103

    13. Preparing for the Future – 113

        Better People – 113

        Better Places – 122

Tables – 133

Diagrams – 133

Bibliography – 133

Index – 135

Preface

Each year students at the university where I teach nominate favorite professors to participate in what is referred to as the *Last Lecture Series*. Of the professors nominated, three are chosen to give public lectures. Each talk should represent the professor's last and final opportunity to speak to and influence students. A few years ago I was nominated. As part of the selection process, I submitted an outline for the lecture I might give. Though I was not one of the professors selected, the outline I created served as inspiration for *Schizophrenic America*.

Schizophrenic America explores the conflict between our American ideals and the realities of our everyday-life. Understanding the origin and nature of this conflict will help us heal our *cultural schizophrenia*, and create harmony for America.

I hope that *Schizophrenic America* will inspire those who read it to live a spirited and unique life among family and friends, while also building healthy community.

Schizophrenic America

Introduction

The more One Knows,
the less One Follows Blindly

A healthy society creates a cultural mosaic in which people are free to express uniqueness, while still participating fully in family and community life. It is fascinating to contemplate how two renown, but contradictory, sociologists, George Herbert Mead and Erving Goffman, might envision a prescription for development of such a society.

Mead believes human beings have a creative inner self, which he refers to as *I*. In contrast, Goffman argues that people are merely actors, learning a script during early socialization, and then playing the role that society requires of them.

In lecture discussions with my university students, most initially agree with Mead. They argue for an *I*, and believe all human beings are unique individuals. Some of the more skeptical and reflective students, however, lean toward Goffman's theory. They worry that people lack a core personality, and are, therefore, incapable of living as a genuine self. Whether students fall into the Mead or Goffman camp, they all express concern about the shallowness they see permeating our society. They agree that unique and meaningful interactions are rare. Most also believe that the way Americans are socialized must change if people are to experience authenticity and uniqueness, and participate fully in family and community relations.

Mead's guidance for social development might involve two steps. First, we must "get in touch with" our *I*, our creative, spontaneous core self. Second, we need to become aware of how our socialization influences us. Mead refers to our socially constructed self image – aspects of our behavior that are determined by social norms – as our *ME*. This *ME* can be considered the "glue" which holds families and communities together. Examination of the *I* typically falls in the realm of psychology, whereas sociologists study the *ME*. A continuous dialogue takes place between these two fundamental components of our self, the *I* and the *ME*. It is reasonable to contend that for Mead, a healthy society creates a culture encouraging harmony in the *I-ME* dialogue – between our core self and social image.

For Goffman, uniqueness and individual authenticity are not possible. Although his view of human beings is cynical, his theory is simple and straightforward. The world is a theater, and human beings play roles according to childhood socialization, and the status they achieve as adults. Healthy societies, Goffman might contend, create cultures where people willingly comply to established social norms and values.

While it might be intriguing to envision a "Goffmanian utopia," *Schizophrenic America* uses Mead's theory to examine those aspects of American culture which trouble my students. Mead might contend that an unhealthy society creates a culture of discord in people's *I-ME* dialogue. The challenge is then to analyze American culture to determine which of its components produce discord.

Incongruence between people's *I* and *ME* causes a split between them, sociologically speaking, a "split social self." The American Psychiatric Association

(APA) does not recognize *I* and *ME* components in individuals. It has, however, constructed a diagnosis for a "split personality," called schizophrenia. Because a "split social self" resembles the APA's definition of schizophrenia, it is useful to study the medical definition of this disease, and then to compare it to a sociological "split social self."

According to the APA, schizophrenia can cause both delusions and disorganized thinking in individuals. Delusions are rigid beliefs that people cling to regardless of obvious contradictory information. These delusions can be religious, grandiose, or persecutory in nature. Diagnosticians must be cautious, however, because it can be difficult to distinguish between delusions and compelling beliefs. Consequently, it is essential to learn exactly how insistent a person is in holding on to a belief, contrary to evidence. Furthermore, if a delusion is considered unbelievable or incomprehensible to cultural peers, the delusion is considered *bizarre*.

This last sentence is important. *Bizarreness* is socially constructed. What is considered bizarre behavior in one culture may be regarded as normal in

INTRODUCTION

another. In this light it is essential to examine the culture of the United States for bizarreness. Do Americans act in bizarre ways, or simply behave according to social norms, or both? Furthermore, it may be essential that an "outsider" analyze our culture, because we are typically "blinded" by our own environment, and therefore, unable to evaluate it from an objective point of view.

Here I will relate a personal story that I feel is relevant. Two years before moving to the United States, I visited as an impressionable young woman in the fall of 1968. Like most Scandinavians I had some knowledge about the country and looked forward to experiencing Hollywood, surfing, and the Flower Power movement in San Francisco. But Scandinavians also knew about race discrimination and the riots in Watts and other large cities. We watched police brutality on TV, and heard that *regular* people carried guns and sometimes shot each other in the streets. We were saddened when president John Kennedy, his brother, Robert, and Martin Luther King were killed. We were dismayed by the ongoing horror of the war in Vietnam. Many Scandinavians believed the United States was still the

Wild West. I came from a country where homicides were rare, and not even police carried guns. I was, therefore, shocked when an American I met said to me "the United States is the best country in the world – God's Country!" I didn't respond. I was frightened when I saw that she was serious. I realized that she had delusional beliefs about her culture, in spite of contradictory evidence. Today, I see that person as suffering from *culturally-induced* schizophrenic symptoms – she exhibited erroneous, religious, and grandiose beliefs.

The phrase "under God" was added to the American Pledge of Allegiance in 1954 during the Cold War. "Under God" was used as political propaganda to promote hostility in America against the atheistic communist Soviet Union. To this end, school children were asked to *blindly* recite the Pledge each day without understanding either its political meaning or that those words violated the First Amendment to the United States Constitution.

The notion of being *blinded* by one's culture is an important concept both in psychology and sociology. For a psychologist like *Sigmund Freud*, socialization is acquired through praise and punishment during childhood. This process, Freud contends, is complete by the age of five, long before children are cognizant of their environment and able to assess what is bizarre about their culture. Thus, their socialization is a subconscious process, potentially "blinding" them to cultural bizarreness. Similarly, sociologists believe children are acculturated by conforming to beliefs and behavior modeled by adults around them. Moreover, if these adults exhibit bizarre symptoms or beliefs, children will unwittingly display the same patterns of bizarreness.

The final point I want to make about medical schizophrenia concerns thought disorder. According to the APA, disorganized thinking can be identified in an individual's speech. For example, a person may skip from one topic to another or make weak associations between ideas, thereby derailing meaningful discussion. Disorganized thinking and loosening of associations have been argued by some diagnosticians to be the single most important features of schizophrenia.

I will once again tie in personal experience. Over the past 15 years I have noticed an increase in "disorganized thinking" among my students. They are more distracted and less able to concentrate on the material discussed in class. When asked to comment on a topic from lecture, many can't organize their thinking or critically analyze the material. They are unable to make associations, to "connect the dots," of the subject matter. If Americans continue to practice fragmented communication at the expense of organized thinking, they may lose their ability to analyze information with a critical mind. If so, they will no longer be able to distinguish between reality and fantasy. In some instances this ineptness could mean the difference between life and death for many Americans.

What is the cause of this "disorganized thinking" among my students? We can explore the answer to this question by making an analogy to medical schizophrenia. Suppose the *culture* in contemporary United States includes a *disorganized thinking* component, producing loose associations – an incongruence or derailment of thought – not only in

Introduction

individuals, but also in our culture as a whole, creating a "schizophrenia" in our society.

To make this analogy, I modify Mead's theory by substituting the *culture* of the United States for the individual person. The *cultural I* in this modified theory represents our core cultural values, such as individualism, liberty, equality of opportunity, knowledge, and spirituality. In contrast, the cultural *ME* can be viewed as an expression of the American way-of-life, or the way we have learned to conduct ourselves in present-day society. We will explore a dissonance in the dialogue between our cultural *I* and our cultural *ME*. This discord in our cultural *I-Me* dialogue encourages disorganized thinking, leading to a *cultural* schizophrenia, a Schizophrenic America.

* * *

I invite my readers to look inside and awaken.

In the first part of *Schizophrenic America* we look at how the norms and values in contemporary United States originated, and then evolved to produce incongruence in our culture.

The second part of the book is about transforming our Schizophrenic America to create holistic well-being for all.

Part I

Our Schizophrenic Malady: Its Origin and Nature

A *culture* is a way-of-life shared by a group of people. Complex societies consist of many types of culture – a cultural mosaic. No single culture can exist in a vacuum. Cultures coexist and are intricately interwoven.

Social scientists divide culture in several ways. They may make divisions based on ethnic background or socio-economic status. Such divisions are of course interconnected. They may also separate culture into material and non-material aspects. Manufactured items, such as clothes, furniture, cars, and computers, are examples of material culture. In contrast, beliefs about right and wrong, beautiful and ugly, good and bad, are examples of non-material culture. *Schizophrenic America* is concerned with non-material culture.

Non-material culture can further be divided into ideal and real. *Ideal* culture, for example, is expressed in fundamental American beliefs – liberty and equality for all; democracy and laissez-faire capitalism; freedom of religion and speech. An example of *real* culture is the American way-of-life.

1
The Cultural *I-ME* Dialogue

Throughout history wise-men and philosophers have "looked inside" to gain knowledge about their inner selves, and about the environment that shapes them. Socrates, who lived in the fourth century BCE, is one of the first philosophers in Western Civilization recorded to have engaged in such an undertaking. While walking the streets of ancient Athens, he and his students philosophized about life and living. *Know Thyself, and Question Your Cherished Beliefs*, he advised.

Over the years I have developed a teaching style based on questioning and critical thinking. Like Socrates, I ask students to engage in *Know Thyself, and Question Your Cherished Beliefs*. Many students are troubled by the lack of self-examination and social inquiry in our society. They recognize that our culture is permeated with inconsistencies and disorganized thinking, and thus they feel disheartened and helpless.

This feeling of paralysis, of being *chained*, was put forth by the French philosopher *Jean Jacques Rousseau* in the mid-1700s. He believed that civilization is the decay of man, declaring that *Man is born free, but he is everywhere in chains*.

Though Rousseau lived in different times, what he said is true for Americans today. The American *way-of-life*, our cultural *ME*, enchains us when it encroaches on our *cherished beliefs*, our cultural *I*. Below I contrast some of the attributes I believe characterize the American cultural *I* with those of our cultural *ME*.

Cultural *I*	**Cultural *ME***
Individualism	Mass-acculturation
Liberty	Conformity
Democracy	Plutocracy
Equality of Opportunity	Social Darwinism
Laissez-fair economy	Economic elitism
Knowledge	Political rhetoric
Cooperation	Competition
Citizenry	Consumerism

It is obvious that the American *way-of-life*, our cultural *ME*, is not congruent with the great principles of our cultural *I*. When there is a schism between what people believe and how they are compelled to act, the likely outcome is bizarre behavior, including disorganized thinking and loose associations. I suggest these behaviors are culturally-induced schizophrenic symptoms.

When I assert that American culture exhibits schizophrenic symptoms, I do not mean to imply that we are individually afflicted with that unfortunate disease. What I mean is that contemporary United States can be viewed as suffering from cultural schizophrenia; most people are socialized to exhibit culturally-induced schizophrenic symptoms.

During the last part of the twentieth century our cultural *I-ME* dialogue became increasingly incongruent, or derailed. One aspect of encroachment by our cultural *ME* on our cultural *I* has been portrayed, accurately I believe, in the award-winning documentary "The Corporation" (Achbar, Abbott & Bakan, 2004). The narrators of this documentary explain that at the beginning of our industrialization, corporations upheld core American values. For example, they initially served the broader community in which they were located. Now, however, corporations commonly exploit employees, and destroy the environment in which they reside. Corporate practice, through mega-mergers, has concentrated power in a monopolistic oligarchy, stripping Americans of a laissez-fair market economy. It is now very difficult for small businesses to be successful. Furthermore, many employees have lost their liberty to bargain for fair working conditions. Plutocracy has replaced democracy; corporations are encroaching on, or crushing, our cultural *I*.

When I show "The Corporation" in class, many students become angry, claiming the film-makers have fabricated information to develop a "negatively biased" view of corporations, and, more importantly, the American *way-of-life*. These students completely avoid or deny the fact that corporations engage in unethical behavior. They have been "blinded" by their socialization and, therefore, are unable to evaluate it from an objective point of view. These students have "learned" at a young age that American corporations are "stellar" because they provide people the opportunity to achieve the American

Dream. Early socialization has "blinded" them to the encroachment of corporations on our cultural *I*.

Sometimes whole societies adopt a "blindness" to the derailment of their cultural *I-ME* dialogue. This became obvious to me after the terrorist attack of 9/11/2001. I was stunned by the inability of so many citizens to "see" how corporate America was using this horrifying event to further their own interests. Moreover, in the guise of patriotic duty and support of our commander-in-chief, this same "blindness" led us into war with Afghans and Iraqis. The term "Axis of Evil," used by George W. Bush, was of course political propaganda. Its intent was to remind Americans of their "Nation Under God," set apart from "evil" nations accused of having weapons of mass destruction. Sadly, few asked why we didn't concentrate our efforts on finding Osama Bin Laden, the alleged organizer of the attack.

Encroachment on our cultural *I* by our cultural *ME* has been promoted more and more by major social institutions. Media conglomerates dominated by power elites saturate us with their "advertisements" daily. Instead of encouraging self-reliance and autonomy in people, they spin information to promote fear and anxiety. These same media giants censor the information we receive through the "news" channels they control. Journalists report opinion rather than unbiased accounts of events. Consequently, much of the political, economic, educational, and religious reporting includes at best only fragmented truth. In fact, our entire culture resembles mere fragments of reality: we serve our children "fragmented" foods instead of whole food products; ads show sexualized body parts instead of whole human beings; students read fragments of books rather than entire works; and families spend only fragmented time together.

How did we *slip off the track*, creating fragmented, loose associations, and disorganized thinking – culturally-induced schizophrenic symptoms? When I discuss this question with students, they seem confused and discouraged. How *did* we slip off the track? One purpose of *Schizophrenic America* is to answer that question.

* * *

THE CULTURAL I-ME DIALOGUE

It is not all gloom, however – after darkness comes sunshine. Americans are awakening; we are at a crossroads. Today many people are well-informed about how the American *way-of-life* is corrupting our government, bankrupting our communities, dishonoring our country, and destroying Mother Earth. Educational documentaries are available on TV and the Internet. Massively open online classes (MOOCs), produced by credible universities, are free to all citizens of the world. We live in the Information Age, and people world-wide are taking the initiative to change the status quo of Mother Earth, practicing sustainable and spiritual living.

2

The Derailed *I-ME* Dialogue

To continue our investigation into *slipping off the track*, let us examine how our cultural *I*, holds up against our cultural *ME*.

If we abandon our *cherished beliefs*, we will draw a blank on who we are and what we stand for. This is dangerous because authoritarian leaders, using media propaganda, might then successfully manipulate our minds and beliefs. We could unwittingly engage in, or condone, behavior which advances only the interests of the power elite. Until the latter half of the 20th century, for example, many social and political leaders asserted that it was morally justified to repress African-Americans and females. Similarly, George W. Bush successfully spun media propaganda and manipulated the American people to wage war with Iraq, even though that country was not responsible for the terrorist attack in September 2001. If Americans begin to actively engage in "cultural" self-examination, they might refuse to be victims of manipulative media propaganda and self-serving power elites.

Our cultural *I* includes *individualism, liberty, equality of opportunity, knowledge,* and *spirituality.* Most Americans agree that these core values are important principles on which to build a great country. Nevertheless, our cultural *ME* – the way we are socialized to conduct ourselves – has encroached on all of these core values. In order to understand how this has come about, we need to consider how our cultural *ME* originated, and the role it has played in denying the majority of Americans fruition of individualism, liberty, equality of opportunity, knowledge, and spirituality.

Our founding fathers, elite White Anglo Saxon Protestants (WASPs), brought the Northern European cultural *ME* with them to the United States. They then modified it slightly to meet the needs of the New World. Hence, their socio-political philosophy reflected Protestantism and English Liberalism. These elite WASPs wrote our Constitution, implemented laws, and developed our economic system. They became justices, lawyers, teachers, bankers, and presidents. The laws initially passed were designed to maintain power for white propertied males. It was the norm that most females and non-whites were barred from voting, getting an education, or holding public office. Today, we still have a white male dominated society. Females and non-whites remain culturally, economically, and politically disadvantaged. Although these citizens have recently seen improvement in their socio-economic status, white males almost exclusively hold top government positions, are the CEOs of corporations, and the presidents of banks. Thus, *equality,* one of the components of our cultural *I*, has never been fully realized in the United States. Instead, our cultural *ME* – the American *way-of-life* – has always encroached on the human rights of non-whites and females, leading to anger and violence in disadvantaged neighborhoods, and to high rates in females of depression and other psychological disorders.

African-Americans and females are not the only people to have been encroached on by our cultural *ME*. *Equality* has been an illusion for a great number of white males as well. Those immigrants who came to the United States during early industrialization to escape religious, political, and economic constraints, often found that *equal opportunity* in the New World was an unrealized myth. They arrived hungry, poor, and unable to speak the language – they experienced a loss of self-identity. The respected sociologist Robert Merton asserts that one response to economic strain is to embrace work ritualistically without questioning work conditions or considering the ethical ramifications of acquiescence. The vigor with which immigrants entered into the industrial work force supports Merton's assertion. They ignored how the cultural *ME* stripped away *cherished beliefs*.

Furthermore, low socio-economic status created a sense of inferiority among immigrants. According to the Austrian psychologist *Alfred Adler*, people compensate for perceived inferiority by striving for "perfection." Obsession with work can therefore be understood as an attempt by immigrants to make up for feelings of inferiority, by creating a "perfect" self-image. In fact, work often became an "escape" for immigrants, providing a desperate hope, while suppressing reflection on their difficult lives. These psycho-social conditions, peculiar to the immigrants, certainly benefited the elite WASPs. They maintained the old European cultural *ME*, with slight modifications. It is unfortunate that immigrants were unable or unwilling to recognize that their way-of-life in the United States did not differ significantly from the European social organization they tried to escape. The initial compliance by immigrants to WASP ideology gave the elite unrestrained power to step-up encroachment on our cultural *I*. This unfortunate situation is an example of derailment of the cultural *I-ME* dialogue.

One of the "spin-stories" fabricated by elite WASPs is the American Dream. It was (maybe still is) a perfect myth, instrumental in maintaining the "Man Against Man" condition in the United States. Rivalry among immigrant groups prevented worker solidarity for many decades. In fact, the willingness of workers to compete with one another, both in the work force, and privately, through accumulation of material goods, was, and still is, held in high esteem. What is more, an inability or unwillingness to compete is regarded as a personal flaw. Thus, a social order similar to the one in Europe emerged, but based on competition rather than social class.

In sum, during early industrialization in the United States, immigrant workers experienced a unique combination of psycho-social factors that gave bang to a zeitgeist which in many ways recreated the old European social organization. The seat of the power elites had changed, however. Today in the United States, corporate CEOs have the same status and power that aristocrats once held in Europe.

It is thus debatable whether European immigrants experienced the freedom they hoped to find in the New World. Certainly they escaped many of the social constraints of their native countries. Their "escape," however, can be compared to the autonomy adolescents seek when they leave home. As adolescents become young adults, their new found freedom from parental constraint is soon replaced with the difficult responsibilities of becoming financially and behaviorally independent. Similarly, immigrants' freedom from the Old World was soon replaced by new psycho-social stress and fear, which led to a growing preoccupation with materialism.

To be viewed with respect, people are forced to follow trends set by the cultural *ME* – a form of mass-acculturation. Conformity has become the American norm. Trendiness is forced on us by TV commercials, fashion magazines, and billboard ads. The majority of Americans are denied the *liberty* to express genuine *citizenry* – to participate as informed members of a civil society.

It is shameful that *knowledge*, another important value contained in the American cultural *I*, has also been crushed by the cultural *ME*. For example, media outlets – owned by a few giant corporations – censor our news, spin the truth, and report only fragments of stories, in order to manipulate, confuse, and entertain the American people. If Americans are in the "dark" and uneducated about the nation's state of affairs, how can they be informed voters and participate in Liberal Democracy? The obvious answer is that corporate leaders and political ideologues do not want the American people to be active participants in our democratic system.

The last factor in our cultural *I* that I want to address is *spirituality*. For me, spirituality includes all the positive qualities that Americans are denied due to encroachment by our cultural *ME*. *S*pirituality is the *liberty* we are given to blossom as unique beings. It is the *liveliness* we feel when we are able to attend to our inner self. It is the *equality* we experience when we can collaborate with our fellow human beings. It is *knowing* that honor and integrity are paramount qualities in our leaders. It is the deep *respect* we feel for all humankind when we are able to respect ourselves. It is the *joy* of spending time with family and friends, and cooking wholesome food together. It is having *fun* and laughing. It is experiencing oneness with *nature* and respecting its greatness. Spirituality *transcends* religious denominations; it *unites* all human beings in a *peaceful* and *free* world. Spirituality enhances our minds and bodies so we can reach a state of holistic *well-being*. Spirituality gives birth to all wonderful experiences.

Spirituality reflects the essential needs of the human core self. A society that puts highest priority on the well-being of its citizens, strengthens its cultural *I* against encroachment by the cultural *Me*. Though citizens of the United States believe in the values embodied in their cultural *I*, in practice few enjoy the benefits of these ideals. The incongruence between our strongly held cultural beliefs and the American *way-of-life* causes serious stress for us all, creating our Schizophrenic America.

* * *

Many Americans are distressed by the dominant role Individualism plays in our society. Though an aspect of our cultural *I*, Individualism acts as a double-edged sword. Next, I will elaborate on this *most cherished belief.*

3
The Birth of Individualism

*You can take people out of a country,
But you can't take that country out of a people.*

Individualism is one of the United States' *cherished beliefs*, a component of our cultural *I*. Core cultural beliefs, such as Individualism, express what the majority of people believe to be an ideal arrangement of a country's society, including the organization of social, political, and economic institutions. Cherished beliefs, or ideologies, differ from society to society and change over time. The ideal of individualism became paramount to Americans during the birth of our Nation.

One aspect of individualism is the opportunity for people to attain personal freedom and happiness. Another aspect is that individuals take responsibility for their own successes and failures. Because the former stresses the importance of meeting one's individual needs, less importance is thereby put on the needs of others. In recent years, for example, individualism has been associated with higher divorce rates and a diminished emphasis on family cohesion. On the other hand, taking responsibility for one's own successes and failures has contributed to the rise of the competitive, distrustful, and aggressive society we live in today. Since individualism leads to such negative social consequences, it is a double-edged sword. Why do we then hold on to it with such tenacity?

The unyielding faith Americans place in individualism is due in part to a "genetic predisposition." Our Northern European forefathers survived centuries of natural selection which encouraged individualism. After the last ice age Northern Europe was settled by small groups of people who survived by hunting, fishing, and collecting seasonal plants. Winters were hard and those who were not prepared perished. Individualism is one outcome of this harsh genetic selection. Europeans brought this characteristic with them when they settled North America.

Agriculture arrived in Northern Europe about 7000 years ago. During spring people planted grains and greens, and in late summer they harvested their crops.

THE BIRTH OF INDIVIDUALISM

If the seasonal yield was lean or failed, people had to contend with little nourishment through the long winter. They adapted to these harsh conditions by developing a frugal and reserved lifestyle, carefully planning their intake of food during times of plenty so that their supply would last until the next year's harvest. Those individuals who planned ahead for meager times survived; the ones unable to do so, often did not.

Consequently, a family system evolved in Northern Europe which favored individual strength, small nuclear kinfolk communities, and monogamy as the marriage pattern. Marriage practices have always been sensitive to available resources at specific times and locations. For example, during economic constraint, the average age of marriage increases, and poor people of both sexes may be barred from marrying and establishing families.

Harsh economic conditions, similar to those that existed in Northern Europe, developed throughout the entire continent during the Early Dark Ages, around 400-500 CE. At that same time, the fall of the great Roman Empire gave rise to dominance by the

Catholic Church for the next millennium. Subsistence living conditions led the church to enforce a monogamous marriage pattern throughout its domain. This pattern remained in effect during the High Middle Ages, circa 1200 CE, even though the standard of living had increased substantially. Monogamy was initially imposed on people to keep the population low, but later it was upheld by the Church to prevent the aristocracy from developing large extended families which might threaten Catholic hegemony. To further diminish the potency of the Aristocracy, arranged marriages between powerful aristocratic families were forbidden. Catholics, however, expanded the nuclear family system, which had been a long standing tradition in Europe, to include extended family bonds and strong community solidarity.

In sum, *ecologically imposed monogamy*, emphasizing individuality, evolved in Northern Europe due to harsh environmental conditions. Later *sociological imposed monogamy* spread throughout the entire continent through Catholic dogma.

The Birth of Individualism

Those people who survived in the cold dark North had acquired their frugal life style prior to the Catholic hegemony. They had experienced starvation regularly and learned to restrain their food intake. Although these people had converted to Catholicism by 1000 CE, they maintained their reserved and sparing lifestyle, thus differing from Southern Europeans, who enjoyed more bountiful living conditions. The dissimilarity between these two cultures resulted in a counter movement against Catholicism in the early 1500s, a Reformation, led by the German monk Martin Luther. Luther's purpose was initially to protest failings he saw in the existing religious tradition. However, when he met with resistance from Catholic leaders, he formulated his own religious ideology. The new faith was referred to as *Lutheran*, or "Protestant" in reference to Luther's protest against Catholic dogma.

Here are some of the most important tenets laid down in the Protestant Churches: a frugal life-style, hard work, discouragement of sexual expression and pleasure, delayed gratification, and, most importantly, never waste time or be unproductive. Protestantism took hold in Northern Europe, precisely because these values were already part of the cultural fabric.

With conversion to Protestantism, individualism took on a new important function. Luther wanted people to establish a personal and exclusive relationship with God. This contrasts with Catholicism, where priests serve as mediators between parishioners and God, and can guarantee salvation to those who repent their sins. Protestants, on the other hand, can never feel certain that God has heard their prayers and forgiven them; there is no one to tell them so.

This new orientation gave rise to a lonesome, unsettling feeling among those who became Protestant. To avert angst and uncertainty many began to preoccupy themselves with incessant work. The warm interactions and community solidarity which Catholicism encouraged were replaced by an "aloneness" affecting both familial and public life. Many immigrants from Northern Europe left their country of origin because they felt a lack of warm family bonds, or a sense of community.

The Birth of Individualism

Protestants who settled North America brought with them a long tradition of individualism, frugality, and belief in hard work (the Protestant work-ethic). This way of life became part of acculturation in the United States, and lasted until the standard of living increased after WW II. In the 1950s, a new lifestyle arose which replaced frugality with affluence and materialism. Corporate America, marketing through mass communication, promoted consumerism while discouraging intellectualism, self-reflection, and citizenry. This new lifestyle, I argue, marks the ascendency of encroachment by our cultural *ME* on our cultural *I*.

* * *

It is interesting to observe how the legacy passed down through the Protestant tradition, which valued individualism and frugality, gave rise to a new cornucopia of consumerism, excess, and group-think. At first glance these two dissimilar orientations to life may appear completely contradictory. In the next chapter I will explain how Protestantism gave birth to capitalism and the consumer driven society in which we live today.

4

Protestantism and the Spirit of Capitalism

In chapter three I explained how individualism initially evolved through natural selection in Northern Europe, and how, during the early 1500s, Martin Luther strengthened individualism by integrating it with Protestantism. Where Protestantism became predominant, people's lives changed profoundly. In fact, according to the famous sociologist, Max Weber, Protestantism slowly transformed the social, political, and economic institutions in Northern Europe, thus paving the way for capitalism.

Henry VIII of England was another player laying the groundwork for capitalism in Northern Europe. Around the same time that Luther implemented Protestantism on the continent, Henry VIII had a falling-out with the Pope in Rome and severed ties with the Catholic church. This break ended a centuries long tradition of shared government between the Catholic church and the aristocracy, and thus gave rise to a new political system in England.

By 1700 an avant-garde socio-political contract had evolved giving rise to *English Liberalism*. Propertied people were now able to choose their leaders and engage in political and economic endeavors. They became "economic beings" – a new power elite – who based their behavior on self-interest instead of religious ideology. Individualism flourished in Northern Europe because it was endorsed not only by the Protestant tradition, but also by the new political system.

It is interesting to observe how radically Northern European culture changed between the Reformation in the 1500s and the Liberal era two hundred years later. Catholicism endorses a socio-political system that emphasizes community, cooperation, tradition, and hierarchy. The new Liberal system, in contrast, stresses individualism, competition, reason, and equality.

Weber asserts that one of the most crucial psycho-social components leading to the transformation from pre-industrial Catholicism to the Liberal era, was the personal relationship that Luther insisted people maintain with God. Unfortunately, it left Protestants feeling uncertain about the probability for individual salvation. To make matters worse, John Calvin, a French theologian and founder of Calvinism, put forth the horrifying tenet of *pre-determinism*. According to him, God determines at birth whether one is saved or damned, much exacerbating Protestant angst.

Anxiety among Protestants, Weber argues, gave spirit to three psycho-social factors which contributed to the European transformation from Catholicism to Protestantism, Liberalism, and Capitalism. Weber's model of the Social System follows:

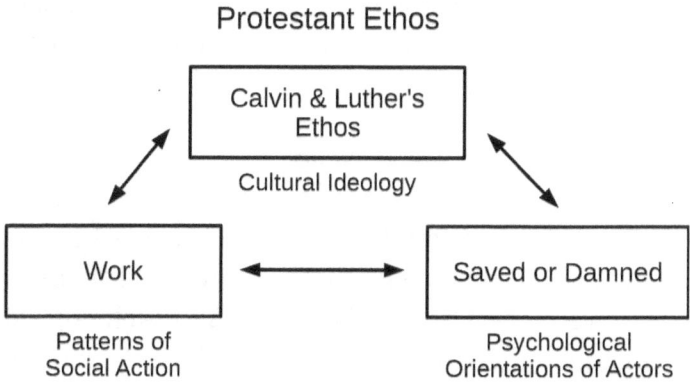

These three factors reinforce each other simultaneously, both clockwise and counter-clockwise, to create synergy within individuals, as well as in the entire society. In the diagram, "Cultural Ideology" refers to the Protestant ethos set forth by Luther and Calvin. The "Psychological Orientations of Actors" corresponds to people's perception of Protestantism. It consists of both a micro or personal understanding, and a macro or cultural understanding, each of which helps make sense of the Cultural Ideology. On the personal level each individual has a unique understanding of what Protestantism means to her or him. On the macro level this component illustrates a collective interpretation of Protestantism as presented in churches, schools, the workforce, and other social institutions.

Weber asserts that the "Psychological Orientations of Actors" component originated as a result of Calvin's doctrine on pre-determinism. People's angst became intolerable not knowing whether they or their loved ones were saved or damned. A psychological orientation therefore developed which identified those achieving material success through work as the saved ones. We should keep in mind that throughout history people in power typically create and implement social norms. Therefore, it is not surprising that the new economic elite rationalized why *they* were the ones to receive salvation.

The third, and final factor in Weber's model is called "Patterns of Social Action." It corresponds to the manner in which Protestants "act out" the Cultural Ideology and Psychological Orientations of Actors components. Considering Luther's tenet that *a waste of time is a deadly sin*, it is understandable that those who had the opportunity and capability, worked hard and followed the Protestant guidelines.

The Protestants' strong work ethic, combined with accumulated wealth reinforced the belief in salvation. That is, the people who were able to work hard, invest in businesses, maintain large bank holdings, donate money to universities, or take on other progressive enterprises, perceived themselves as the "saved" ones. This idea thus reinforced the Psychological Orientations of Actors that the new economic elite were the ones to receive salvation. Moreover, during the industrializing of England the new economic elite were also able to replace the church and the aristocracy to take the social, political, and economic power.

People who embodied the Protestant ethos began to enjoy high status and respect in society. In contrast, those who failed were seen as outcasts. In fact, they were often perceived as sinful and unworthy of pity. The Protestant movement had created a division between people based on physical and mental prowess, and simple good fortune. It was a brutal consequence of Protestantism. People's status was no longer based on deep faith, but on their capacity to work hard and achieve monetary prestige.

When the new economic elite replaced the hegemony of the church and aristocracy, the archetypal Protestant ethos, including pre-determinism, vanished. However, the belief in hard work and accumulation of material goods continued to be an important force for emerging Liberals to maintain their superior status in society. In addition, the attitude toward poor people changed. They were no longer viewed as damned, but instead were perceived as lazy and stupid folk to be exploited as the rich saw fit.

PROTESTANTISM AND THE SPIRIT OF CAPITALISM

One can compare the transformation of Europe from early Protestantism to Liberalism with America's shift from early Puritanism to modern consumerism. In Europe, once the secular replaced the sacred, economic affluence replaced a pious life-style. While this same transformation took place in the United States, I argue that a more *negative* change occurred in our culture. We allowed corporate America to infiltrate our democratic system and "buy off" government representatives. Consequently, Americans have lost confidence in their political leaders' commitment to uphold our cultural *I*. Corporate America dictates a form of mass-acculturation while dumbing down the American *way-of-life*. Instead of feeling proud of their uniqueness, people have become insecure and, therefore, obsessed with "fitting in" or being "plugged in" to escape anxiety.

* * *

How did this transformation come about? I think it is partly because we have allowed unrestrained capitalism in America. In the next chapter I will briefly describe how capitalism originated in Europe and was then adapted to the United States, creating a system which has allowed corporate America to dictate our political and social lives.

5

Fostering the Growth of Capitalism

In this chapter I will briefly explain how capitalism originated in Europe and later was adapted in the United States. As discussed in the previous chapter, capitalism arose from the Protestant spirit, and gained strength during England's industrialization in the mid-1700s. Capitalism had a violent beginning. The emerging economic class, then referred to as the Bourgeoisie, passed laws to drive farmers and rural artisans off their land. Homes were burned and fields enclosed to raise sheep. The dispossessed peasants were forced to move to the cities where living conditions were unhealthy and inhumane.

When the rural population lost their livelihood, they became dependent on the Bourgeoisie for work. Farmers and artisans became a new class called the Proletariat who worked in factories owned by the Bourgeoisie. Unfortunately working conditions in the manufacturing plants were dreadful. Young children and adults worked 12-14 hours per day, yet barely made enough money to survive.

Karl Marx devoted his life to improvement of the working conditions for the Proletariat in Europe. He urged them to form strong alliances and rebel against the Bourgeoisie. While this effort was initially unsuccessful, workers eventually formed strong unions and gained political power. After two world wars devastated Europe and left her people in ruin, the working class became even more powerful. Today, all European countries have strong political labor parties which guarantee employees good working conditions and ample wages.

In Western Europe and Scandinavia these powerful worker coalitions were effective in creating an economic system referred to as Welfare Capitalism. This type of economy guarantees provision for people's most basic needs. It offers universal healthcare, free education, even at universities, generous disability and unemployment insurances, paid maternity leave for up to one year, and inexpensive or free child-care. Where Welfare Capitalism is the norm, self-interest and competition are encouraged. People have private ownership of businesses and enjoy personal profit. These countries have high Gross Domestic Product (GDP) and low income disparity between rich and poor. While people pay high taxes for these ample benefits, they repeatedly vote to maintain Welfare Capitalism, endorsing liberal benefits for all members of society.

In the United States the history of capitalism took a different path. During our early industrialization, capitalism was adopted in this country. However, worker solidarity, instrumental in the evolution of capitalism in Europe toward Welfare Capitalism, did not occur in the United States. Though workers attempted to unionize, each new wave of immigrants arrived poor and hungry. They broke strikes-lines and offered to work for lower wages than established workers. Consequently, for many decades salaries remained modest and employee benefits were almost non-existent. Experienced workers either moved westward or agreed to work for the same low wages the new immigrants accepted.

The existing contention among immigrant groups was often exacerbated by the long traditions of strong national pride these people brought with them from their countries of origin. Social integration, referred to as the "melting pot," is for the most part a myth.

The conditions that emerged between immigrant groups were more like *War With Man Against Man*, a sentiment put forth by the sixteen century British philosopher Thomas Hobbes. The separation between immigrant groups is still visible in major cities such as New York and Chicago, where people settled in enclaves according to nationality and interacted with "others" only on an as needed basis.

I believe that the lack of solidarity among the immigrant workers was detrimental to the American working-class. The new economic elite were able to implement political and economic laws that benefited themselves, while experiencing little or no opposition from their employees. Consequently, the United States does not have a political labor party to represent the workers. It is the only country in the Western civilized world that does not offer universal healthcare and some form of paid maternity leave for new mothers. Meanwhile, the cost of a college education increases yearly, the middle class is shrinking, and upward mobility is becoming more difficult.

FOSTERING THE GROWTH OF CAPITALISM

Nevertheless, people failing "to get ahead" are frequently seen as "losers." The tenacity with which we hold on to this idea is impressive. This is partly due to the American Dream, a vision put forth by the economic elite during our early industrialization. People who subscribe to this idea believe that achievement is possible for all, and that we all get what we deserve – Americans who work hard will become respectable, affluent citizens. Our Protestant socialization, which encourages hard work and accumulation of wealth, made the American Dream an easy sell.

While some Americans do achieve the American Dream, most peoples' tireless work-effort does not increase their standard of living. The idea of living the American Dream creates destructive competition, which leads to a distrusting work force lacking in social reciprocity. Individualism and isolationism are increasing while families and communities suffer. American workers miss out on building strong communal and social bonds; a condition that diminishes their political strength against corporate hegemony.

It is fascinating to reflect on the acculturation of the American people and inquire into the psycho-social factors that make them so tolerant of political and economic oppression. Many feel indifferent about social and political issues and are unwilling to engage in dialogue concerning the well-being of our country. This is especially bewildering given that the United States was born from people who fought to become independent from England, and later nourished by immigrants who rebelled against the status quo of their native countries.

* * *

Why do so many Americans now experience apathy and indifference? I argue that it is because we suffer from culturally-induced schizophrenic symptoms. The derailment of our *cherished beliefs*, our cultural *I*, by the American *way-of-life*, our cultural *ME*, has resulted in a disorganized thinking pattern. More and more, people find it difficult to patiently concentrate on subject matter or practice critical thinking. These skills are essential for analysis of topics concerning the well-being of our country. Next we will continue our *journey inside* and *awaken* to new psycho-social factors causing Americans to lose sight of their duties as citizens.

6

Social Darwinism

I argue throughout this book that Americans experience incongruence between strongly held cultural ideals and the American *way-of-life*. This is partly because our cultural *ME* was originally designed to maintain power for white propertied males, and supported *equality of opportunity* only for them. Though upward mobility nowadays is possible for more than just white males, many Americans still find it nearly impossibility to lift themselves out of poverty. Poor people are typically unable to compete with those from the middle and upper classes.

A social system founded on competition is, generally, as unjust as one based on a class or cast system. In fact, for the most part, it propagates the status quo of society. That is, the rich stay rich and the poor remain poor. Rich families can afford to give their children a superior education. In contrast, children from poor families often receive substandard schooling. Rich people network with each other to get the best jobs. Poor Americans work for minimum or below minimum wages. Equality of opportunity is still a myth.

People who are well educated and hold good jobs are considered the *fittest*. In contrast, the poor, the disabled, and disadvantaged minorities, unable to compete in society, are frequently regarded as *unfit*. Being poor is considered by many a personal flaw. Some Americans believe that the poor get what they deserve in life.

The sociological notion of being the *fittest* originated with the English philosopher and sociologist Herbert Spencer. He lived during the 1800s, when Britain was a world power. Spencer coined the phrase "survival of the fittest." For him competition, both between individuals and between organizations, was essential to assure that the *fittest* people and institutions evolved. These ideas are referred to as Social Darwinism. "Survival of the fittest," however, typically favors the power elite. They have the monetary, political, and military power to get a head start and stay ahead of others.

SOCIAL DARWINISM

According to the American sociologist C. Wright Mills, the power elite in the United States are the industrial corporations, the military-industrial-complex, and the executive branch of the U.S. government. In terms of Social Darwinism, these institutions have acquired *fittest* status. I argue that they also have been reinforcing the encroachment of our cultural *ME* on our cultural *I*. In so doing they have impinged on our democracy as well, and reinforced the class system in the Unites States

When I lecture on Herbert Spencer, students agree that competition is a valued component of the American *way-of-life*. Many of them, however, are troubled by our Social Darwinist acculturation. They learned as children that the United States is *the land of the free* and *home of the brave*; where everyone, through hard work, can attain the American Dream. Then, at the university level, many students become disillusioned with what they have earlier been taught. They realize that the ideals they learned when young are disregarded in American daily life. They worry they won't be able to find a good job to become financially independent and pay off their college debt.

I will modify Max Weber's model, described in chapter four, to illustrate the role of Social Darwinism in our society. In the diagram below, I have replaced his original factors with the psycho-social factors I believe most accurately depict our culture. These factors create the stress and disillusionment my students and many other Americans experience.

Social Darwinism

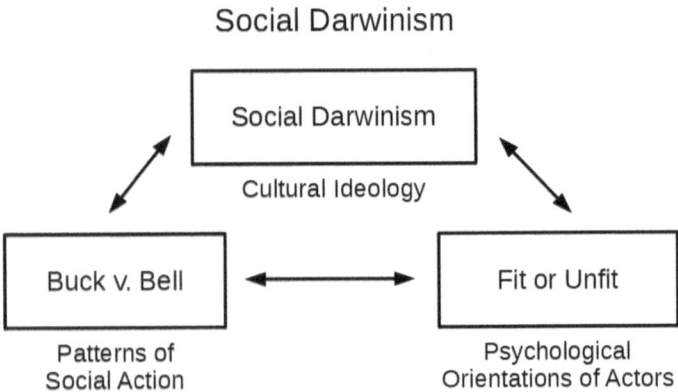

Again these three factors reinforce each other simultaneously, clockwise and counter-clockwise, creating a synergy within individuals as well as in society as a whole. I suggest that our Cultural Ideology, while incorporating both our cultural *I* and cultural *ME*, mainly consists of the *ME*, because the *I* has been encroached upon; Social Darwinism eclipses Equality of Opportunity, thus becoming the principal aspect of our Cultural Ideology. Americans are socialized to strive for *fittest* status. While this is impossible for most of us, we hold on to this idea as though religious dogma.

The "Psychological Orientation of Actors" component represents people's interpretation of Social Darwinism both on a cultural and personal level. For example, culturally we are driven to work hard, accumulate material goods, and appear youthful and attractive. If we do not attain these criteria we are *unfit*, and may even be held in contempt by the *fittest*.

On a personal level the majority of Americans also endorse Social Darwinism, although some 'out-of-the-ordinary' people reject it. Hippies of the 1960s rejected Social Darwinism. *Freegans*, a more current sub-culture, subscribe to anti-consumerism as one way to escape our cultural *ME*. They work less and build communities based on sharing and caring for others. Such sub-groups are often scorned by the main culture. Consequently, those who succeed in attaining personal and cultural freedom typically experience some psychological anguish in the process.

The third factor of this model is "Patterns of Social Action." It illustrates the manner in which Americans "act out" Social Darwinism. In the extreme, consider the United States Supreme Court decision Buck v. Bell in 1927. In that decision the Court ruled that it was legal to permit compulsory sterilization of the *unfit* in an attempt to improve the gene pool. Today, that decision draws much criticism and has been compared to eugenic programs in Nazi Germany.

Where Social Darwinism rules, an *unfit* status is determined by political, economic, and cultural attitudes. To be declared *unfit* in the United States has changed since Buck v. Bell in 1927. Social Darwinism in contemporary United States may be most visible when we examine childcare policies. For example, we tolerate that one in five children falls below the poverty line. In fact, the standard of living for American children ranks below that of Canada, Australia, New Zealand, Japan, and almost all of Europe. Furthermore, the United States is one of a handful of countries in the entire world which does not have some form of extended maternity leave. This same Social Darwinist attitude has led to a lack of adequate health and dental care for poor children. The educational system has also failed poor children. Even the much touted No Child Left Behind Act of 2002 was a failure in raising academic performance for most children. As adults the *unfit* population is unable to compete in the labor market, further increasing their *unfit* status. Finally, without appropriate resources to change their status, many *unfit* people end up incarcerated, kept out of sight from the *fittest*. It is therefore not surprising that the United States has the highest rate of incarceration in the world. More troubling is that one-third of all violent crimes are committed by youngsters under 18 years of age. Our Social Darwinism has resulted in a lack of empathy toward the most vulnerable individuals in our country. As we have seen, this lack of empathy leads to many serious sociological problems.

I believe our unwillingness to help the poor is a remnant of our Calvinist heritage. Poor people are judged as *unfit* and thus unworthy of equal opportunity. In terms of the cultural *I/ME* concept, acting out Social Darwinism can be seen as reinforcing the encroachment of our cultural *ME* on our cultural *I*. In doing so, the cultural *ME* has impinged on our cherished beliefs; the democratic system, equality of opportunity, liberty, and cooperation.

Only through perpetual advancement and competition do people attain *fittest* status. This is often a grueling undertaking, and many people have to suppress their most praiseworthy human qualities in the process. Trust, kindness, cooperation, and respect are not suitable attributes in our competitive world. In contrast, mistrust, disrespect, aggression, and competition are qualities encouraged when profit is the only goal. Furthermore, corruption, lying, and cheating have become normalized behavior as an outgrowth of Social Darwinism.

Thus, people acquire negative emotions, such as fear, sadness, and anger. They fear that someone else will surpass them; they are sad, having lost their most precious human qualities; they are angry because society values those younger, smarter, richer, and more attractive.

SOCIAL DARWINISM

Social Darwinism jeopardizes the physical and mental health of all Americans. Doctors medicate those people who are most afflicted by this social illness, treating the symptoms rather than the cause. The extent of this problem is clear. Millions of Americans take prescription drugs in order to cope. Millions more self-medicate in an attempt to manage daily living. In the process many become addicted to alcohol, prescription or street drugs.

If the United States wants to act as a role model for the rest of the world, we must try hard to eliminate Social Darwinism from our Cultural Ideology, the American *way-of-life*. Unfortunately, many Americans are reluctant to relinquish the "survival of the fittest" attitude. They have learned to believe that every American is responsible for his or her own successes and failures. Those who succeed in achieving the American Dream are considered the *fittest*. Successful Americans, however, are rarely self-made individuals. They are raised in well-to-do families who help them attain success. They live in safe environments, eat healthy food, go to elite schools, and get superior healthcare. Affluent people network with each other to secure well-paying jobs.

Thus, becoming *fittest* involves many people, as well as favorable socio-economic conditions. For most Americans, however, aspiring to the American Dream is a grueling process, a nightmare. It demands a great deal of work with little or no chance for success, nor time to reflect on the health of our Nation – a high price to pay.

* * *

We tend to look outside for approval and self-worth. Failing to achieve the American Dream makes us feel less worthy than those who succeed. If we look inside, we can awaken to maturity and responsible self-reflection. It might then be possible to turn the American Dream into a new *way-of-life* where sharing, caring, and tolerance become *fittest*.

7

The Aesthetic Stage

Who looks outside, dreams;
Who looks inside, awakes
– Carl Jung

There are many reasons that incongruence exists in the American cultural *I-ME* dialogue. In this chapter I suggest that Americans tend to *look outside and dream*, simply because they are "adolescent." The United States is a young country; an adolescent New World. An older country, like older people, may turn from *looking outside*, to *look inside*, and *awaken* through introspection and reflection.

Considering that countries consist of individuals, one could argue that societies evolve through stages of development analogous to human beings. It might, therefore, be possible to apply developmental theories for human beings to entire countries. Philosophers and social scientists have formulated theories on the development of both human physiology and cognition. I will examine the cognitive development of the United States' culture utilizing a theory formulated by the Danish existential philosopher Soren Kierkegaard.

Kierkegaard asserts that children and most young adults exist in an Aesthetic stage of development. Aesthetic individuals are self-centered, focusing on the sensual pleasures of life, and want immediate gratification. Some individuals remain in the Aesthetic stage throughout their lives. Others, however, advance to an Ethical stage. In order to make this transition an individual must become bored and dissatisfied with Aesthetic living.

In contrast to aesthetic individuals, ethically oriented people are outward-looking and believe in upholding the norms and values of society. Teachers, judges, community planners, and religious leaders are typically in the Ethical stage. They willingly forgo self-centered gratification to collaborate with others to make an orderly society which runs smoothly.

When I lecture on Kierkegaard, I ask my students to extend his theory of stages and apply it to countries instead of individuals. The consensus is that the United States has an aesthetically oriented culture.

THE AESTHETIC STAGE

My students argue that immediate gratification and self-centered behavior are paramount in American culture. We are a young country, the adolescent New World. Our acculturation is for the most part based on self-centeredness, immediate gratification, and the sensual pleasures of life. Like teenagers we flex our muscles, show off our strength, and are preoccupied with physical prance and beauty. Television programs and popular magazines encourage aesthetic living. They promote fantasy and illusion. Superficiality is favored over philosophical contemplation; youthful reactiveness is preferred to mature reflection.

Adolescent culture is a doubled-edged sword. It brings an energetic sense of invulnerability that is seductive and exciting to many; but it also brings feelings of insecurity and fear, as well as uncertainty of identity and lack of self-confidence. For example, Americans can be consumed by fear. After WWII, we feared communists, socialists, and civil rights activists. As those threats faded we began to fear feminists, and we still worry about homosexuals, liberals, right wing conservatives, religious fundamentalists, and, again, socialists. There are boogie men around every corner. Unfortunately, this combination of eagerness to flex muscle, a culture of fear, youthful naivety, and a sense of invulnerability has resulted in horrific domestic and international policy making. The wars in Vietnam, Afghanistan, and Iraq are recent examples.

Our aesthetically oriented culture wobbles between "fight" or "flight" behaviors. Like adolescents we struggle to create an identity and are driven by peer-group conformity and mass-media acculturation. Like adolescents rebelling against their parents, we rebel against our European "parents."

* * *

Many Americans, however, have become bored with or feel victimized by Aesthetic living. The United States is at a cross-roads, seeking a new identity. I believe our country is beginning a transition into an Ethical stage of development. We must be cautious, though, and work hard to stay the course. History tends to repeat itself – we must protect our Nation against harmful social factors which might jeopardize cultural maturation. Next, we look at history. I will show that the United States, regardless of change, has stayed the same.

8

History Repeats Itself

*Those who do not study history
are condemned to repeat it.*

If public policy makers want to create a society in which people can experience uniqueness and authenticity, they must study social history. If they neglect to do so, they may overlook important factors which could impede social improvement. The origin of social problems must be understood to avoid undesirable conditions in the future.

In the United States, policy makers need to carefully analyze our history to effectively direct transformation into an Ethical era. I believe Industrialization, and more recently, Globalization, are the two most important periods in our history. I have created a simple comparison of these two periods. I call it "History Repeats Itself":

Industrialization	**Globalization**
Sweat Shops	Sweat Shops
Worker Alienation	Social Darwinism
Impoverished Workers	Impoverished Workers
Robber Barons	CEOs
Concentration of Wealth	The One Percent
Monopolies	Merger Mania
Unregulated Capitalism	Unregulated Capitalism
Great Depression	Great Recession

It is obvious that past problems continue to plague us in the present. When I lectured on the topic "History Repeats Itself" in the Spring of 2008, I originally put question marks where you now see Great Recession. I was not surprised when our economic melt-down occurred in the Fall of that year – history *does* repeat itself.

One reason Industrialization is so important in the history of the United States is that millions of immigrants settled here during that period. These immigrants helped establish the socio-economic conditions that are still part of our country today. For example, the lack of solidarity between groups of the European immigrants hindered the creation of unions and a political Labor party. This lack of collective power kept workers impoverished for many years. Moreover, it allowed the elite to legislate economic policies that established unregulated capitalism. The combination of alienation among immigrants and unrestrained power of the elite was partly instrumental in creating conditions which led to the Great Depression. Many of the factors seen under "Industrialization" have reoccurred during Globalization.

In his book *Collapse*, Jared Diamond studies positive conditions that help countries sustain viability through time, and negative conditions that cause societal collapse. Diamond suggests we pay close attention to the history of social thought to prevent a collapse of the United States. He argues that the increased division between rich and poor we see in our country is an imminent danger. In contrast to the majority of our citizens, wealthy people often live in gated communities, dine only in expensive restaurants, attend elite country clubs, and rarely befriend people of low socio-economic status. If they remain isolated, Diamond continues, collapse is inevitable. That is, if the rich do not experience, or at least appreciate, the problems of other citizens, they will not be motivated to help solve those problems.

Diamond suggests that we learn from Europeans. They gave up their cherished nationalism in order to prevent a WWIII. Similarly, the United States should renounce consumerism, individualism, militarism, and aggressive foreign policy in order to prevent collapse. It is remarkable that the behaviors Diamond wants us to renounce are the same behaviors our Aesthetic Darwinist culture tends to foster. They will be difficult to give up.

Paleoconservatives argue that many of our current social problems are caused by outsourcing the majority of manufacturing to low income countries. After WWII blue collar workers in the United States were able to establish strong unions and receive respectable salaries with benefits. As a result of outsourcing, however, they are now losing well-paying jobs and are forced to work in the low pay service sector. In 2013 the rate of pay for CEOs at the 350 largest public U.S. firms was 300 times that of typical workers in those firms. This is a ratio 15 times larger than it was in 1965, before outsourcing of manufacturing jobs began. To continue in Diamond's line of thought, if outsourcing of production caused socio-economic losses for CEOs, as it has for blue collar workers, CEOs would lobby to bring production back to the United States!

The problem with outsourcing can also be viewed from a different perspective. Although European countries have also outsourced much of their production, the working class has been protected by Labor parties. I believe a strong political labor party in the United States would be effective in improving blue collar workers' socio-economic conditions.

Meanwhile, the state of affairs continues to worsen for Americans. First we saw an increase in the price of food, gasoline, and housing. Then, after the economic meltdown in late 2008, socio-economic problems arose resembling those of the Great Depression of the 1930s. More than a third of our children live in low income families. Even though the unemployment rate has fallen since the end of the Great Recession, the majority of jobs created have been in the low paying service sector. Such occupations rarely offer benefits, such as employer healthcare, paid sick leave, or time off for new mothers. This is regrettable. Americans are hard working people and deserve better living conditions than they currently have. We must appeal to the elites and hope they can find compassion for average citizens. Americans are often innocent victims of greed, and of self-centered economic and political policy making. Hopefully, compassionate leaders will come forth to help solve the problem of disparity of wealth. If elites are unwilling to cooperate with the rest of the American people to make the fundamental changes we need, the result will be continuing economic decline, leading to widespread poverty, and associated violence and crime.

Many of my students are apprehensive about graduation, and entry into the labor market – competition is grueling and well-paying jobs are scarce. Meanwhile, educational requirements for workers have increased. Today, a four year college degree carries the same status that a high school diploma did in the 1950s. But high school is free, and university tuition has skyrocketed. Many graduating seniors now have college debt of $30,000 or more. The transition into adulthood is more difficult for students today than for their Baby Boomer parents. Some students might still be paying for college loans when they reach retirement! We are exploiting students. They deserve the same living standards that their Baby Boomer parents have, and educational opportunities matching those of their European counterparts.

The old European power system has been recreated in the United States, but with power players changed from monarchs and aristocrats, to corporate CEOs and wealthy oligarchs. Like kings, CEOs have isolated themselves from the population they are supposed to serve. This isolation led to the economic meltdown in 2008, and is the reason we have not yet fully recovered; many new jobs are of poor quality.

In the decades following the economic collapse of 1929, Franklin Roosevelt and then Lyndon Johnson were able to improve economic conditions for Americans by legislating the New Deal and the Great Society. Once the working class finally made economic progress, however, the Reagan administration began chipping away their benefits. Beginning with Reagan, democracy has slowly been replaced by plutocracy and crony capitalism. Economic policies now mainly benefit the rich, and only the rich feel empowered by our Plutocracy. They are either involved with policy making, or have connections to those who craft legislation. In either case, they have noticeable control over law-making.

In contrast, main-stream Americans feel disempowered. They have lost confidence in our democratic system. They experience *taxation without representation*. They were unable to halt Reaganomics, and powerless to stop jobs being shipped to low wage countries. When workers lose employment, they lose employer health insurance, the ability to fund a pension, and, most importantly, hopes and aspirations for the future. This state of affairs is a vicious cycle which widens the gap between rich and poor in American. If Americans want Liberal Democracy instead of plutocracy, they must rebel against *taxation without representation*. Remember the Revolutionary War! *Taxation without representation* has returned. History *does* repeat itself.

9

Sacred versus Secular Life

In the 1200s the European theologian St. Thomas Aquinas integrated the secular and sacred worlds in a Great Synthesis. The function and meaning of this synthesis was to promote the "good society" on earth. Aquinas believed that in a society where public policies are crafted on religious ideology, people will think and act with virtue. As a result everyone will go to Heaven after their time on earth ended.

Henry VIII ended divine government in the early 1500s when he created an English church independent of Rome. As a direct consequence, the basis of political power changed from sacred to secular. When church rule declined, the self-interest of a new elite class became dominant.

The 1700s Scottish economist and social scientist Adam Smith worried about how people would form moral judgment during the rapid expansion of the labor market in industrializing England. Exploitation and degradation of the lower class became rampant.

Capitalists perceived workers simply as economic assets. While Smith was realistic, he was also hopeful that an *invisible hand* would produce unintended social benefit from selfish individual actions. While the term "invisible hand" has been interpreted to mean laissez-faire capitalism, I prefer the more poetic interpretation, that is, "an order established by Nature and God." I think Adam Smith hoped that his "invisible hand" would keep society functional and balanced – a perspective similar to that of Aquinas.

Like Adam Smith, it is possible that our Founding Fathers also hoped that an "invisible hand," the Hand of God, would bring order and prosperity to the fledgling New World. This sentiment is epitomized by the phrase "In God We Trust" which was placed on United States coins in the mid-1800s. Even so, our Founding Fathers insisted that our country should have a wall of separation between church and state. The Supreme Court of the United States has repeatedly referred to the phrase "separation of church and state" in case rulings.

Exclusive secular sovereignty, however, has never governed this country. Our social, political, and economic policies and institutions reflect the struggle between Christian values and capitalistic business ideology. Why haven't policy makers in the U.S. been able to integrate these two spheres of our culture? One explanation is that business interests have had nearly unrestrained power to create a secular world ruled by their self-interest. The tension between our sacred and secular worlds has led to political and economic damage.

Below I list some factors representing traditional Christian ideology (our sacred realm of life) with corresponding factors representing the present American *way-of-life (*our secular life).

Sacred Life	**Secular Life**
Thou Shalt Not Kill	Death penalty
Anti-militarism	Militarism
Forgo possessions	Consumerism
Compassion	Competition
Community	Individualism

The behaviors shown under "Secular Life" are both encouraged and rewarded in contemporary United States. Traditional Christian values as seen under "Sacred Life" have slowly eroded. Many of my students are distressed when they see the stark contrast between our Christian values and our *way-of-life*.

St. Thomas Aquinas asserted that public policy can be beneficial when based on Christian ideology. While our policy makers from time to time have tried to convince themselves, and the rest of the world, that the United States is founded on religious ideology – "One Nation Under God," or opposition to an "Axis of Evil" – it is instructive to see if it is possible to align our secular and sacred lives.

Individualism, listed under "Secular Life," comes at a great price. We inherited this trait from our Northern European ancestors. Individualism was initially "geographically induced" to survive the cold climate in the North. Later, Individualism became part of the Protestant ethos, thus "reinforced" by the Reformation. The necessity of Individualism has changed in present-day United States. First, we have plenty of food to feed every American. People go hungry because of political and economic decisions. For example, farmers are paid by the government to reduce production to keep crop prices high. Second, most Americans do not follow a strict Protestant ethos as a guideline for living. As a result, Individualism is not an ideology we need to emphasize, either as a *cherished belief* or in our *way-of-life*. Instead, we should encourage community solidarity as a priority.

Another important psycho-social factor mentioned above under "Secular Life" is *Competition*, an aspect of capitalist economies that is strongly emphasized in the United States. But many Americans are burned-out by continuously competing with their fellow citizens, sometimes to the point of "stepping on" others in order to get ahead. If we encourage *Compassion* over competition, the United States will enter a much more humane era. In addition, our cultural schizophrenia will weaken once our sacred and secular spheres are integrated. Thus, *Love Thy Neighbor As Thyself* will become both attitude and conduct, reflecting a Nation balanced by an *invisible hand*.

Northern European countries have replaced Individualism with Communality and Compassion, aligning public policy with Christian values. These countries have implemented Welfare Capitalism to provide for people's most basic needs, such as universal healthcare; generous disability and unemployment insurances; maternity leave; and free or inexpensive child-care. When the role of Competition is reduced in the United States, Americans will receive similar benefits. This is essential! Many Americans unwittingly neglect the well-being of their family, their environment, and themselves because Competition is primary to our *way-of-life*.

It is disconcerting that most Americans are unaware of how harmful the American *way-of-life* is. Why are so many blind to the negative effects of Individualism and Competition? One reason is that we value high socio-economic status, which we think can be acquired through Individualism and Competition. We should instead learn to respect people who contribute to the physical, spiritual, and mental well-being of ourselves, our fellow citizens, and our communities.

Finally, let's consider *Militarism*. The United States maintains armed-forces superior to any in the world. To sustain our *military industrial complex* and be ready for war at all times, we need a reservoir of "disposable" young people. Many come from poor and violent neighborhoods. During childhood they are hungry and angry. They receive an inferior education and have little or no hope for a prosperous future. In order to survive in their neighborhoods they must adopt tough and aggressive behavior. They lack self-worth and are held in contempt by others. Many of them join the military to escape poverty. They displace their anger and aggression onto our "enemies." They are willing to give up their lives for the United States, even though their country fails to attend to their most basic childhood needs. More than a third of the children growing up in the U.S. live in poverty or low income families. Does the United States, a rich country, discourage Commonality and Compassion in order to maintain a supply of "disposable" young soldiers? This is a question worth considering.

* * *

I believe aligning our sacred and secular worlds would promote an integrated society, and reduce our cultural schizophrenia. But is such an alignment possible in the United States? Are Americans ready for change? Is the young generation powerful enough to dismantle old, harmful beliefs and habits? Is the Baby Boomer generation willing to assist the young in building a new, flourishing United States? We live in a tumultuous time, but it is also an exciting time. Our country has been a place where dreams do come true, and impossibilities become possible. A call for many *invisible hands* is in order to help restructure our cultural mosaic.

Part II

A Holistic Reorientation to Life and Living

In this section, we will once again *look inside*. We will examine and reframe our cultural beliefs to create harmony between our cultural *I* and cultural *ME*, thus "curing" Schizophrenic America. Only then will we *look outside and dream* – to imagine how individuals can become Better People, who will create Better Places where holistic well-being is the norm.

10

Reframing Our Protestant Ethos

If the United States is to flourish, we need to implement new and effective socio-economic policies. To prepare, we must first evaluate existing cultural factors. As we continue our journey into the twenty-first century, attitudes and behaviors which were useful at the birth of our Nation may no longer be effective. We also need to educate the American people about the benefits of policy change. In this chapter I will once again discuss our Protestant heritage. This is important because I believe Protestant socialization is the root of many psychosocial ills in contemporary United States.

Our country was established by White Anglo-Saxon Protestants. The U.S. is founded on the Protestant ethos — *hard work*, *accumulation of wealth*, and *individualism*. These values helped immigrants survive and prosper during our Nation's formative years. These same values, however, have also fostered a deep sense of insecurity in both rich and poor. Many rich compare themselves to their peers and feel inferior if they are unable to keep abreast. The poor, on the other hand, often feel disillusioned and hopeless because they are unable to get ahead. To try to escape inferior status, they typically work very hard, harder than any other people in the Western world. They begin a competitive journey in Kindergarten and continue on into old age. Many are on an endless treadmill, buying stuff they can't afford in an attempt to create a respectful image. Unfortunately, their anxiety rarely subsides and they frequently feel empty inside.

Early Protestants believed that *a waste of time is a deadly sin.* As a result, "unproductive" activities, such as playfulness, generosity, and enjoyment of sexual pleasure, were looked upon as sin. Wasting one's time was interpreted as 'don't be intimate and don't experience joy', thus reenforcing hard work, accumulation of wealth, and individualism. Our commitment to uphold the Protestant ethos, however, is destroying our families, our communities, and undermining our Nation as a whole. Over recent decades, we have seen a reduction in social cohesion and community participation. Americans have fewer friends and less social support than people in most other countries. Many have experienced a diminished sense of happiness and well-being.

In the 1950s, corporations began to tap into the anxiety and boredom felt by many Americans. Businesses hired psychologists to help them exploit the insecurity people felt. Ads were displayed in newspapers, magazines, and billboards promising people confidence, happiness, and personal success once they began to buy products, regardless of utility or need. And so it happened that little by little Americans were turned into "shopaholics." Consumerism superseded citizenship. Today, people of all ages are seeking immediate gratification on smartphones, or in shopping malls, instead of participating in family and community gatherings.

Social-psychologists have studied Americans to see if happiness and success have increased since our "endless shopping spree" began. To date, all research confirms that desire-shopping does not lead to personal success or happiness. In contrast, when people replace intimacy, family fun, and spiritual living with self-indulgence in shopping malls, or plugged-in, a diminished sense of well-being and joy results.

Americans have been manipulated by shortsighted and dishonest corporate practices since the 1950s. It is time we awaken to how we have been victimized, and how the most vulnerable members of society suffer the most. In the spirit of materialism, we have unwittingly neglected our children. For example, it has become common practice for Americans to "farm out" their children to daycare centers or nannies. This is partly due to the "necessity" for multiple jobs to support consumer driven habits. In other words, it has become more desirable to accumulate stuff than to raise one's own children. It shows how far removed we are from our basic instinct, to nurture and care for our children.

In many counties today women work outside the home in order to boost their household economy. As a result, social policy makers in both developed and undeveloped countries have implemented paid maternity and/or paternity leave. This allows parents to bond with their newborn children, and helps ease family transition. The United States, however, is one of the few countries that does not mandate paid maternity leave.

Though Americans as individuals might be caring and compassionate toward children, our social policies tell a different story about the value of family in our country. Sadly, Americans consent to childcare policies far inferior to those demanded by people in other developed countries. The state of affairs for children in the United States is heartbreaking! One in five lives in poverty. These children are denied a healthy start to living. I believe Americans have neglected the welfare of their children, families, and communities, in pursuit of the Protestant ethos: work hard, accumulate wealth, and practice individualism.

In order to nourish our families and communities, we need to reframe our Protestant ethos. All major religions are founded on the supremacy of compassion. To reframe our Protestant heritage, we must align our sacred and secular spheres of life. When compassion and community replace competition and consumerism, something "magical" can happen in our cultural mosaic. We might reassess the "dark" side of our Protestant heritage. Words like *poverty, idleness,* and *leisure* would no longer invoke contempt.

Poverty, for example, is a relative term. Americans are building bigger houses, but their families are getting smaller. They have more "gismos" to play with, but less time to enjoy them. Many people live in big houses filled with material goods, but they experience poverty in their hearts. Economic *poverty,* however, is usually not caused by idleness or wasting time. Globalization and automation have reduced job opportunities. Decent jobs are hard to come by, so even "respectable" college graduates often experience economic poverty. Once we realize that economic policy in the United States is unfavorable for most people, I believe the word *poverty* will no longer be associated with contempt. Once compassion and community have replaced competition and individualism, the majority of Americans will help each other build strong sustainable communities, abundant in camaraderie, work, and joy.

Idleness also evokes contempt in most Americans. When they hear that Europeans have six-weeks paid vacation and additional paid public holidays, many

Americans poke fun of them. Idleness, however, is both healthier and cheaper than using alcohol or drugs to cope with our stressful lives. Idleness is essential to replenish the body, the spirit, and the mind.

Finally, *Leisure* is a bad word in our vocabulary. Family leisure is almost a rarity in today's dual-career families. If parents do have "spare time," they fill it with busy-ness, such as taxiing children from one event to another. Leisure, however, is essential for human beings! People who set boundaries to insure uninterrupted leisure – stillness to "catch up with themselves" – are healthier and more spiritually fulfilled than those who are always on the run. Leisure should be practiced both in one's home and in nature. A walk in nature can quickly lift one's physical, emotional, and spiritual well-being. People living in large cities should make it a priority to escape into the wilderness as often as possible. According to Richard Louv, an expert on *Nature Deficiency Disorder* (NDD), most city dwellers suffer from NDD. He argues that people who are deprived of contact with nature, have higher rates of obesity and depression, which he sees as symptoms of NDD. In addition, children suffering from NDD display diminished creativity compared to children who play freely in nature. Human beings are Nature-beings, and when they forget, they are less likely to rejuvenate and energize themselves.

Idleness and *Leisure* are aspects of R*ecreation*, that is *re-creation* – rejuvenating one's physical and spiritual being. Recreation does not have to be expensive. Recreation includes walking in a park, sitting under a tree in green foliage, or watching waters flow in a fountain. Reframing our deeply held Protestant ethos will contribute to well-being for our bodies and minds.

* * *

Perhaps our younger generations already question the validity of our Protestant heritage. After all, the social and spiritual landscape of the United States is rapidly changing. Let's now continue our journey into the twenty-first century, and awaken to new ideas which might help eliminate our cultural schizophrenia.

11
Revolutionizing Our Cultural Mosaic

It is my experience that many young people today want to see radical change in the socio-political system of the United States. But they do not know how to begin or whom to turn to for help. They feel helpless and hopeless. Many of my students say they want to do something heroic, something noble, something larger than their own individual concerns.

I have spent many hours with these "students of change." I listen, I encourage, and sometimes I make suggestions. I tell them a favorite proverb, "a good person is someone who always tries to become better." I point out that a country is really nothing but individuals connected through interaction with one another. Thus, social change can happen automatically – one person at the time – if we all try to become better people.

These ideas are especially relevant when we discuss Competition versus Cooperation, and Individualism versus Community. Students realize that our country will benefit if Americans adopt a cooperative attitude and build healthy communities, yet they still favor competitive individualism. Competition is of course as deep-seated in the American psyche as individualism. I suggest that those of us (myself included) who have individualistic and competitive traits, can redirect these traits beneficially by becoming involved in self-betterment. This praiseworthy task requires *internal* competitive-individualism. When we exert competitive energy improving ourselves, it is much easier to engage in cooperative behavior with others.

I am reminded of a legend about an old Cherokee Indian discussing inner conflict with his grandson. There are several versions of this legend. Here is the one I feel is most appropriate for this chapter.

> "There is a fight inside me," the Cherokee said to his grandson, "a terrible fight between two wolves. One wolf is evil – he is anger, envy, and sorrow; arrogance, greed, and self-pity. The other is good – he is peace, love, and joy; humility, kindness, and compassion. This same fight is going on inside you, too, and inside every other person."

The grandson thought about what he had heard, then asked, "Which wolf wins?"

His grandfather replied, "The one you feed."

Cooperation and community are essential to human cultures everywhere. In United States, however, we emphasize competition and individualism, a latent consequence of our Protestant ethos. If we want to revolutionize our cultural mosaic we must selectively feed cooperation and community, not competition and individualism.

It is unrealistic, however, to expect all adults to "feed" cooperation and community, especially since many have been encouraged to behave otherwise since childhood. We might, therefore, consider yet another approach to the issue of social change. We could teach our children the value of cooperation and community.

That has already begun. But if we wish to revolutionize our cultural mosaic, more is needed. I suggest a new, revolutionary, social movement. The United States has recently supported two such social movements. First there was the Civil Rights Movement in the 1960s, and then the Feminist Movement in the 1970s. These movements came about through the *Cooperation* of millions of individuals who wanted to make better *Communities* in the United States.

Now it is time to embark on a *Children's Rights Movement.* Child advocacy groups need to stand up for the rights of our children. We must guarantee that all children have the nurture and protection they need.

To ensure that infants have a healthy start to life, quality prenatal care must be made available to all mothers-to-be, regardless of socio-economic status. In the United States the infant mortality rate is higher than in Europe, Japan, Australia, Canada, and even Cuba. This is, in part, due to a lack of adequate health care for pregnant women.

Paid maternity leave must be mandatory. Intimate bonding between mother and child, including an extended period of breastfeeding, is important to *lifelong* health and well-being. A year or more of maternity leave is common in other developed countries.

Poverty must be eliminated. In 2014, one in five children in the U.S. lived in poverty, and many more lived just above the poverty line. This is unconscionable considering that the United States is the richest and most powerful country in the world. Where poverty is common, infant mortality is high. Lacking paid maternity leave, poor mothers must return to work soon after giving birth. Many leave their newborns in childcare nurseries where exposure to communicable disease can be high.

Physical illness is not the only problem our healthcare systems must deal with. Many children of working parents are placed in childcare centers for most of their waking hours; others become latch-key children, fending for themselves for extended periods of time. Such circumstances can be stressful and have negative effects on a child's psychological well-being.

According to the Surgeon General, twenty percent of children in the United States suffer mental health problems, a number that is increasing. ADHD and other behavioral disorders are most common. Mood and anxiety disorders are also common. In addition, the rates of eating disorders and drug addiction are rising. Sadly, suicide is the leading cause of death among teenagers and young adults.

The United States must implement comprehensive preventive healthcare and welfare programs for children and young adults. Many of those suffering from mental health problems don't receive adequate care. As a result, they may have low educational achievement, or drop-out of school all together. Unfortunately, many youth with mental health disorders end up in the criminal justice system. This is especially dangerous. Placing groups of at-risk youth together, propagates delinquency. Once youth have had a brush with the criminal justice system, they can be greatly disadvantaged. It can become difficult to find good employment and lead a fulfilling life. Relapse into the criminal justice system is common.

In the United States more money is spent imprisoning our youth than attacking the root problems of poverty and mental health. We are more willing to punish our children than provide them a chance at life.

A good person who always tries to become better must demand that we the people of the United States *cooperate* to develop first-class welfare programs for our children, and build healthy communities for them to grow up in.

Ode to a Child

A Child is a miracle, indeed
So vulnerable, so innocent, so sweet
A child needs care and protection
Daily love and affection
Every child needs a chance to discover
Freedom, equality, regardless of color

Be patient, don't rush me
I have my own way
I need time to flourish
Tranquility where I stay
Today is my journey
Tomorrow may be too late
Please, don't make me wait

SCHIZOPHRENIC AMERICA

Why is the wealthiest country in the world unwilling to provide even the most basic care for its children?

***

It is not just our children who are cheated out of the right to holistic well-being. We all are. Many Americans have lost touch with Mother Nature, and therefore lack respect for living things. We pollute the air and waterways, we poison our food supply, mistreat the animals we eat, and consume unwholesome food. We are leaving a terrible legacy for our children and our children's children. We must ask ourselves: Why are we willing to tolerate this sad fate? The viability of our country depends on inspired dialogue among all Americans – everyone is responsible for assuring that the United States has a safe and prosperous future. We want our country to flourish!

12
I People and *Me People*

A student recounted this story in one of my classes:

> I went to the advisement center yesterday and waited about 20 minutes to be seen. There were a dozen or so other students waiting, all plugged in to some type of electronic device! Even though, as university students, we had a lot in common, no one talked. Everyone was focused on their e-device. It was eery!

He continued:

> I was the only student who wasn't plugged in, and that was just because of this class. I was observing and thinking about social behavior.

This student was referring to class discussions related to the *plugged-in* generation. Today, youngsters are plugged into entertainment devices much of the time, and therefore, rarely ask themselves: *Who am I?* or

What is going on around me? They are disconnected from their core selves and from each other.

Here I am reminded of "secondhand desire," the idea that we obsessively look outside to satisfy our need for passion, opening ourselves to manipulation, deadened to genuine passion.

In our media driven society we are disconnected from what we should be most connected to: ourselves, each other, and our environment. Our neighbors can help us build healthy sustainable communities. Mother Nature provides us with the air we breath, the water we drink, and the food we eat. Every one of us must get involved in preserving Humanity and the Earth; we must breath energy and vitality into everything that exists, not unwittingly destroy it all.

At my university we teach a course called Modern Social Problems. We need to expand instruction and discussion beyond the university. The time has come to create a class for everybody called *Ongoing Social Spiritualism*. It should be offered in a mass open-ended format, where *all* Americans are invited to participate. The purpose will be to discuss how best to connect to each other and to Mother Nature. The hope is that everyone will take responsibility for their choices, to disconnect from secondhand desire and get on-board with Ongoing Social Spiritualism. At that point, we will awaken to a new Earth where secondhand desire has been replaced by social spirituality.

What content should be included in Ongoing Social Spiritualism classes? Allow me to return once again to my university students. I often hear them using the term "cutting loose" when they talk about partying and feeling free. Unfortunately, many of them have to be inebriated to "cut loose" and experience the happiness of freedom. I think it is partly due to our Protestant culture, haunting us in many obscure ways, telling us that freedom is a *waste of time* and *a deadly sin*. Americans need to "cut loose" from their Protestant chains and learn that *freedom can bring joy*, with no need of drugs or alcohol. Freedom allows us to "unfold."

One can "cut loose" and "unfold" through meditation, or by simply strolling in nature. Meditation helps us center on our Core Self, and Mother Nature rejuvenates our spirit. Many healthy activities are inexpensive, and don't leave us with hang-overs the next morning. We cannot start soon enough!

When I lecture on the topic of "cutting loose" and "unfolding," I refer to G. H. Mead's theory of the social self, discussed in the Introduction. Mead suggests that all human beings consist of two components: an *I* and a *ME*. According to him, the *I* is unseen to the public. It is our creative, spontaneous core self. Some might consider it the soul. In contrast, the *ME* is our social image; the aspect of ourselves which is seen in public. A metaphor for the *I* could be the flame of a candle: the fire which gives us life and spirituality. I argue that most people in the United States have an underdeveloped *I*. They live in a helter-skelter world, rushing from one activity to the next, rarely pausing to "get in touch with" their *I*. They do not have an opportunity to develop their creative and spontaneous core self. They are too preoccupied to become truly spiritual. Furthermore, I believe that people with an underdeveloped *I* suffer from anxiety, stress, and depression. They try to escape such feelings by clinging to rigid forms of socialization, or by turning to drugs or alcohol to "cut loose" and glimpse their *I*.

I trust that children will develop a strong *I*, if given time and space to frolic in nature, if allowed alone-time without the distraction of media entertainment. They will develop creativity, spontaneity, and spirituality while building a solid sense of character. Such children are less likely to be manipulated by others, or caught up in mass-acculturation. They will become *I people*.

I people are creative, spontaneous, and spiritual in character. They conduct themselves according to the spiritual and moral code, *Love Your Neighbor Like Yourself*, the foundation of all major religions.

In contrast to the *I*, or core self, the *ME* is our cultural self. It refers to the way people conduct themselves. *ME* "contains" the way a person is socialized or instructed to act by family, religion, and the secular culture in which they reside. I believe that most Americans have a *ME* exhibiting Individualism, Competition, Consumerism, and Militarism. Such behaviors are not representative of *I people*. I argue that people who exhibit these characteristics have an underdeveloped *I*. I call them *ME people*. Their *I* has been deadened by mass-acculturation.

The command *Love Your Neighbor Like Yourself* implies empathy. According to Webster's College Dictionary, empathy is the identification with or vicarious experiencing of the feelings, thoughts, etc., of another. Empathy stems from the Greek word empátheia which means affection.

I people are empathic people. They have affection for their fellow human beings and feel the pain and joy of others. For *I people* it is a calling to build healthy communities and eliminate violence and suffering. Once *I people* gain more influence than military leaders, the world will change. *I people* need to come forward to show the way. They are so desperately needed. Every American has the obligation to free their *I* from the limitations of their *ME*. They must join other *I people* to transform the American *way-of-life* from one where conflict and war are glorified, to one which canonizes sustainable living and world peace. A new Cultural Ideology will emerge founded on the spiritual principle, *Love Your Neighbor Like Yourself.*

All human beings have a genetic predisposition to be empathic people. According to social scientists, this natural inclination toward empathy can be nourished in children by the love and care of adults during the first few years of life. It is, therefore, paramount that the United States implements compassionate childcare policies. We must no longer suppress our children's *I* by exposing them to mass-acculturation. Too many of them have already been sacrificed to Individualism, Competition, Consumerism, and Militarism. This might not be obvious to some, but I detect it when I see...

> a small child hurried from activity to activity, or rushed off to some ad hoc childcare center. I hear in their cry: Don't interrupt me. I'm not finished. Give me time and space to create the unique person I can become.

I see an adult crying. I listen, and I hear...

> because I was constantly interrupted as a child, I suppressed my *I*, my chance to create a true

unique self. I began to lie to myself, and then I misled others. I became part of the herd, the mass-acculturated. But I feel something inside me, something trapped which wants to "cut loose." But still I hurry from activity to activity, unable to listen to my *I*, my true unique self.

I see a homeless person in the street. I see their humiliated and broken body crying...

> I have been deceived by others. I have deceived myself. I turn my eyes away from you in shame. I am without an *I*. I'm empty inside.

The following statement has been attributed to George Bernard Shaw:

> *Life isn't about finding yourself.*
> *Life is about creating yourself.*

I think this statement correctly reflects a need of all human beings – to be granted time and space to create the wonderful unique person that their *I*, their illuminating flame, can inspire.

I People and Me People

I often remind my students of the lyrics from The Star-Spangled Banner: *O'er the land of the free and the home of the brave*. These lyrics are inconsistent with the experience of most Americans, who are not free, but are chained by the herd mentality of mass-acculturation. People blindly engage in Individualism, Competition, Consumerism, and Militarism, never stopping to ask why.

I hope each American will become insightful and brave enough to let their *I* develop, to engage in creative self-growth and enjoy freedom. Americans will then experience a fresh new world; one seen from their *I*, their unique point-of-view.

* * *

Classes in *Ongoing Social Spiritualism* will help Americans envision a new holistic culture, one conducive to the development of *I people*. The United States will become a place where the spiritual principle, *Love Your Neighbor Like Yourself*, is practiced in *a land of creative joy* and *a home of true freedom*.

We have looked "inside" and awakened to the state of affairs in our contemporary culture. In the final chapter we will look "outside" and dream about creating *Better People* and *Better Places*.

13

Preparing for the Future

Better People and Better Places

*Before we can accomplish something
We must dream it*

Better People

Throughout history people have dreamed of a better world – in song, poetry, and letters. In ancient Greece, Plato dreamed of a utopia where ethics and justice eliminated evil. St. Thomas Aquinas envisioned an ideal society based on Christian values. More recently, Martin Luther King dreamed of an America where all brothers and sisters walk hand in hand. Personally, I dream of a country where *I people* live freely in harmony.

What stands in the way of dreams coming true? I think the answer is that people are afraid of the unknown. We fear change, and thus seek security in the belief that our culture is superior to others; we embrace the culture we are born into, and desperately defend its traditions despite obvious social failures.

Today, the United States is at a crossroads – change is in the air. Consequently, people are afraid. Not knowing what the future will bring provokes anxiety. Those who benefit from the status quo worry about losing their benefits. Those who don't benefit also worry, afraid things will get worse. Adopting a new *way-of-life* is unsettling.

It is essential to dream, to imagine a new culture that benefits everyone in the United States. We need to design a sustainable culture consisting of *Better People* and *Better Places*. *Ongoing Social Spiritualism* classes will help accomplish this.

In theory, creating a new culture in the United States is simple. We need to replace our incongruent cultural *I-ME* dialogue, which encourages "disorganized thinking" with one promoting congruence and harmony. Thus, our behavior, our cultural *ME*, should reflect the ideals of our cultural *I*. In addition, we should encourage Americans to develop a strong individual *I*. In practice this task might seem overwhelming. Yet, now is the time to let go of the past and create the future.

First, the past no longer exists. The United States has gone through many fundamental socio-economic changes. Initially, most immigrants who came here were farmers. Agriculture was then a labor intensive occupation requiring many people to cultivate the land. Industrialization superseded agriculture. As a result, labor shifted from farm to factory. Machines and assembly-lines "took" jobs away from artisans. Globalization and post-industrial technology are eliminating even more jobs. Both blue and white collar workers see their jobs outsourced to low income countries. Many of the remaining jobs are being automated. Meanwhile, the population in the United States is growing; we will have less work and more people. This will force Americans to create a new *way-of-life*.

Second, the zeitgeist, or spirit, in which the United States was born is out-of-date. Early colonists depended on a strong work ethic and a frugal individualistic lifestyle to overcome the difficulties in settling the New World. In contrast to early colonial times, there is now an abundance of food and sufficient technology to feed, clothe, and house every American. Yet, our Protestant zeitgeist tells us it is wrong to do so. As individuals we may wish our fellow human beings to have food, clothes, and safe living conditions, but our *way-of life* denies these basic needs to many. The American zeitgeist is obsolete! It needs to be modified. Why wouldn't we want all Americans to experience the abundance this country has to offer?

If we do not prepare for the future, the United States might see an unemployment rate matching that of the Great Depression within a few decades. During that time, 30 to 40 percent of the population were without work, and many experienced extreme poverty. As we have recently witnessed in the Middle East, such conditions give fertile ground for revolts and civil wars. If Americans turn a blind eye to obvious socio-economic and spiritual failures in this country, the same might happen here. It is my hope that dreamers will be able to peacefully guide us to a new *way-of life*.

Preparing for the Future

To prepare for the future we must bring congruence to our cultural *I-ME* dialogue – we must free ourselves of cultural schizophrenia. To begin this healing, Americans must acknowledge "disorganized thinking" as a symptom of our cultural schizophrenia. This process can be catalyzed through discussion in the *Ongoing Social Spiritualism* classes. We must all engage in transforming our culture, and awaken to the freedom that comes with evolving into *I people*.

If we are to create a new *way-of-life*, we need to ensure that our educational system encourages creativity and flexibility. Students must learn to "think outside the box." This is essential. Today, blue- and white-collar work is increasingly automated or outsourced to other countries. Everyone now needs to reinvent themselves!

I talk with my students about which jobs will remain in the United States, and which will be automated or outsourced. This is important information for them. They want to learn skills which will be useful once they graduate. Students wish to be in control of their future – to be captains of their own ships. After years of financial dependence on parents and student loans, they wish to be independent and self-sufficient. They need satisfying, productive work. Once Americans become *I people*, I believe we will create a country where satisfying work is available to all.

How will we achieve this goal? Ideas will be suggested and developed through discussion in the *Ongoing Social Spiritualism* classes. It is important that planning be transparent. Ideas will then be tested at the local community level, and, if successful, implemented more broadly.

I people will be at the forefront of our transformation. Once respect for *I people* becomes greater than respect for warriors, more and more Americans will ride the *I Wave*. To paraphrase John Quincy Adams, we must "inspire others to dream more, learn more, do more, and become more."

Our transformation has begun. Many young Americans already ride the *I Wave*. They are creative entrepreneurs; they value freedom and prefer small local work-settings; they create individualized products to sell in their local communities, or advertise one-of-a-kind merchandise on the internet for purchase by other *I oriented* people.

The shift into our new paradigm will unfold in many parts of our cultural mosaic. Investment in education, however, should be a priority. Adults, as well as children, should be educated about the benefits of reframing our cultural *ME* to design a new *way-of-life*. To this end, education centers should be located on nearly every street corner. Unused buildings can be remodeled and utilized for *Ongoing Social Spiritualism* classes. Renovation of empty buildings will create many temporary jobs to help ease the transition into our new way-of-life. Intense labor will be needed to help re-create the United States and produce *Better People* and *Better Places*.

Schools for young children would be called *Kindergarten Kindness Clubs*. Students will be placed in small classrooms, designed to be spiritually uplifting. The ratio of students to teachers must be small. Such clubs will be win-win for students, teachers, parents, and the community. Children will receive individual attention, and the space and time to create their *I*. The hurried child syndrome, so common in contemporary United States, will no longer be acceptable in our new way-of-life. Each hour of the day should be considered a gift for children to evolve into the *I people* they are meant to be.

Kindness Clubs for grown-ups will also be available. Many adult Americans currently suffer symptoms of mass-acculturation: anger, anxiety, stress, and hopelessness. Kindness Clubs will provide support groups and peer counseling for adults to join. *Ongoing Social Spiritualism* classes will help participants understand the transition from *ME people* to *I people*. They will be encouraged to cut loose from the herd mentality, and experience the meaning of becoming *I oriented*. For some this process will seem frightening. But through re-creation of ourselves, we will feel a surge of well-being. Once released from mass-acculturation, we will ride the *I Wave*.

Those staffing the *Kindness Clubs* will be holistically oriented, *re-creational* therapists. Enrollees will be able to study topics which can help them become *I oriented* and prepare for the future. Sessions will be created on an as-needed basis and might include, for example, physical education, food planing, gardening, animal farming, and parenting skills.

Children and adults joining in *Kindness Clubs* will experience improvement in their physical, mental, and spiritual well-being. This will not only help us individually, but will benefit our country as a whole. Resources currently allocated to healthcare and our prison system will be released to fund the *I Wave – Better People and Better Places*. Furthermore, employers will notice that the labor force is becoming healthier. Workers will take less sick leave, and productivity will increase. The *I Wave* will be a win-win *way-of-life*.

Corporations should also prepare for the new paradigm. Like other historical transformations – the agricultural era, industrialization, and globalization – the *I Wave* is inevitable and unstoppable. Corporations should, therefore, embrace the *I Wave*, and enlist an *I oriented* workforce. Once they get onboard, CEOs of such corporations will realize that the new paradigm is a win-win business deal. They will invest both time and money in *Kindness Clubs* to help create *Better People and Better Places*.

Better Places

> *When the Power of Love Overcomes*
> *the Love of Power there will be World Peace*

I think this message is the secret for creating Better Places. When respect for *I people* surpasses respect for military leaders, there will be world peace. *I people* are empathic people. For them it is a calling to build healthy communities, to eliminate violence and suffering. It is in the interest of every human being to awaken to the freedom and creativity of their core self, to become *I people*! *I people* will build Better Places to create a peaceful world.

Before we can hope for world peace, we must work to eliminate human misery everywhere. Where there is suffering, violence is prevalent, and assault on innocent people is common. Even the best law enforcement agencies or intelligent services in the world can not prevent such attacks. We recall the terrorist attack in the United States on September 11, 2001. That disaster broke the hearts of all Americans, and the rest of the world mourned with us.

I am reminded of the Bee Gees song, "How can you mend a broken heart?" Can we mend our hearts and start living again? I believe we can. First, all nations must assist in mending the broken hearts of the oppressed and poor. The top priority of every country should be to end suffering and violence. When human beings live in a healthy environment, they respond by becoming empathic and peace-loving. We must all assist in building Better Places so everyone can live again. This will not be as difficult as we might expect. The Nobel Peace Prize recipient Albert Schweitzer once said: *The only ones among you who will be truly happy will be those who have sought and found a way to serve*. I believe that human beings are hard wired for sociability, attachment, affection, belonging and empathy. It is, therefore, possible to build an empathic civilization where human beings connect to one another. It sounds simple – I think it is. I am reminded of another song from my youth, The Beatles' "All You Need Is Love." *Love* leads to empathy, the only human attribute which can save us from destruction.

When people live in Better Places, they collaborate with one another to preserve the well-being of their neighborhoods. They prefer to support local businesses instead of buying merchandise from big-box stores. They become locavores by favoring foods bought at their local farmers' markets. When neighborhoods are carefully maintained, inhabitants learn to honor and respect all living things. People arrange block parties and potlucks to connect with each other. They recognize that communities founded on friendship and cooperation are communities without violence and aggression.

Better neighborhoods will have strong local relationships, reminiscent of small pre-industrial villages. But in our current post-industrial era, where access to the Internet is the norm, people are also connected to distant places. In that respect, *localization* and *globalization* exist side by side. People will live in their local "village" and at the same time be citizens of the world.

Once people are socially connected, both locally and globally, a new cultural ideology will emerge. It will be based on the spiritual message common to all major religions: *Love Your Neighbor Like Yourself*. Because localization and globalization exist side by side, *your neighbor* can be someone living next door, or someone from a distant place, perhaps a person you met while traveling abroad, or someone you befriended through social media.

Max Weber's model of society, introduced in Part I, provides a perfect template for designing Better Places. In the figure below I have revised Weber's model to fit the new *localization-globalization* paradigm:

Spiritual Unification

```
                    ┌─────────────────────┐
                    │  Love Your Neighbor │
                    │    Like Yourself    │
                    └─────────────────────┘
                       Cultural Ideology

  ┌──────────────────┐                    ┌──────────────────┐
  │ Functional Ethic │ ◄────────────────► │ Intrinsic Ethic  │
  └──────────────────┘                    └──────────────────┘
     Patterns of                             Psychological
     Social Action                           Orientations of Actors
```

In the original model the Protestant Ethos was the Cultural Ideology. I have replaced it with the all encompassing Cultural Ideology: *Love Your Neighbor Like Yourself*.

The psychosocial factor called "Psychological Orientation of Actors" represents people's positive mental attitude and confidence in their Cultural Ideology. Children will be socialized to understand that Love Your Neighbor Like Yourself is a fair and logical way of thinking. This socialization will be emphasized in the Kindergarten Kindness Clubs, and later reinforced in churches, schools, and community centers, as well as through global citizenship.

Finally, the psychosocial factor referred to as "Patterns of Social Action" represents a new local-global way of acting, reinforced by both the Cultural Ideology and the Psychological Orientation of Actors. Public policy based on Love Your Neighbor Like Yourself will be acted out on a global scale, once citizens of the world understand such policy is logical and fair.

While Weber created his model of society in the early 1900s, ancient Greek philosophers were already familiar with the connection between people's psychological orientation and subsequent social action. Aristotle, who lived in Athens in the fourth century BCE, suggested that two types of ethics arise from that connection: functional ethic and intrinsic ethic. In the revised model above, Functional Ethic refers to the *activities* people engage in which support Love Your Neighbor Like Yourself. Intrinsic Ethic refers to the positive *feelings* which grow within individuals when they behave in ways which support Functional Ethic. The act of building Better Places in society is an example of Functional Ethic. An example of Intrinsic ethic is the joy people experience when building Better Places and loving their neighbors.

Today, psychologists believe Intrinsic Ethic is associated with high self-esteem in individuals. When people support a cause they believe is morally just, it is a joy to do so, thus improving their self-esteem. The connection between functional ethic and intrinsic ethic, or *doing good* followed by *feeling good*, is a common feeling among human beings. Once *doing good* is associated with "I love my neighbor like I love myself," *feeling good* about loving one's neighbor will then follow. The reverse association, *feeling/doing*, is also a common experience. If people feel good about themselves, they may act upon that feeling. For example, "I love my neighbor like I love myself" may be acted out by organizing a potluck or giving money to a favorite charity.

The three psycho-social factors in Weber's revised model reinforce each other both clockwise and counter-clockwise. This is depicted in the figure by the doubled headed arrows between the three psycho-social factors. Because the factors reinforce each other both clockwise and counter-clockwise, they create a synergy within each individual, and in the entire world as well. Once that synergy has been established it will be impossible to stop.

Once Love Your Neighbor Like Yourself is accepted as the norm, both individually and globally, a congruent dialogue between *feeling good* and *doing good* will create an *I Wave* for the world. This *I Wave* will transform human culture. Humanity may not survive unless we start this process now. The United States should be a role model. The rest of the world is watching. Where we lead, the global community will follow. Imagine the joy of riding the *I Wave*.

* * *

We the Individual
Brought up by the Media
Brainwashed to feel Special
Lost Among the Masses
Fragmented and Frustrated
Pause!
Be Present, Wonder
Meditate on Meaning
Wish for Wholeness
Center and Create
I over *ME*

* * *

Tables

Cultural *I* vs Cultural *ME* 16
Industrialization vs Globalization 70
Sacred vs Secular 79

Diagrams

Protestant Ethos 43
Social Darwinism 58
Spiritual Unification 125

Bibliography

Goffman, Erving. *The Presentation of Self in Everyday Life*. Garden City: Doubleday, 1959.

Mead, George H. *Mind, Self, and Society*. Chicago: University of Chicago Press, 1934.

Smith, Adam. *The Theory of Moral Sentiments*. Edinburgh: A. Millar, A. Kincaid & J. Bell, 1759.

———. *The Wealth of Nations*. London: W. Strahan & T. Cadell, 1776.

Spencer, Herbert. *Social Statics*. New York: Appleton-Century-Crofts, 1851.

Weber, Max. *The Protestant Ethic and the Spirit of Capitalism*. New York: Scribner, 1930.

Index

Adler, Alfred..............................26
aesthetic stage.....................65, 66
American Dream..........27, 53, 57, 63, 64
American Psychiatric Assoc.......5
American way-of-life.........11, 16, 25, 47, 55, 79, 108
Aquinas, St. Thomas...77, 80, 113
Aristotle...................................126
Beatles.....................................123
Bee Gees.................................123
Better People...................113, 114
Better Places...........122, 125, 127
bizarreness....................6, 7, 9, 17
bourgeoisie..........................49, 50
Buck v. Bell..............................60
Calvin, John..................43, 44, 61
Capitalism....49-51, 70, 71, 78, 82
Cherished beliefs.........15, 16, 23, 26, 33
Cherokee story.........................96
Children's Rights Movement....98
core personality...........................4
core self.........4, 30, 105-107, 122
cultural *I*............16-19, 23-25, 27, 33, 85
cultural *I* vs cultural *ME*...16, 133
cultural *I-ME*........15, 19, 27, 114, 117
cultural *ME*.......16, 19, 23-27, 55, 62, 114, 119
cultural mosaic....3, 13, 91, 95, 97
delusional beliefs........................8
Diamond, Jared...................71, 72
disorganized thinking.......6, 9, 10, 15, 17, 20, 114, 117
economic elitism.......................16
English Liberalism..............24, 42
ethical stage.......................66, 68
fittest..................56, 57, 59, 61-64
Founding Fathers.................24, 78
freegans.....................................59
Freud, Sigmund......................8, 9
functional ethic.......................127
Globalization......69-71, 115, 124, 125, 133
Goffman, Erving..............3-5, 133
Goffmanian utopia......................5
Great Depression................70, 71
Great Recession...................70, 73
Great Society............................75
Henry VIII............................41, 77
history repeats itself............69, 70
holistic reorientation.................85
I oriented..........................119-121
I people..........103, 107, 108, 113, 117, 118, 120, 122
I Wave..............118, 120, 121, 128
I-ME dialogue..........5, 15, 17, 19, 23, 27, 65, 114, 117
idleness................................92-94
In God We Trust........................78

INDEX

incongruence......5, 10, 17, 30, 55, 65, 114
individualism.........16, 24, 33, 38, 41, 42, 79-82, 95-97
Industrialization......28, 51, 69-71, 133
intrinsic ethic..........................127
invisible hand................78, 81, 84
Johnson, Lyndon.......................75
Jung, Carl..................................65
Kierkegaard, Soren....................66
Kindergarten Kindness Clubs....... 119, 126
Kindness Clubs................119-121
laissez-faire capitalism..............78
leisure...................................92-94
liberal democracy...............29, 76
localization.......................124, 125
Love Thy Neighbor...................81
Love Your Neighbor.......107-109, 124-128
Luther, Martin.........37, 38, 41, 44
Marx, Karl................................50
mass-acculturation.......16, 29, 47, 107-109, 120
ME people...............103, 108, 120
Mead, G. H........3-5, 11, 106, 133
Merton, Robert..........................26
military industrial complex.......82
Nation Under God..............19, 80
nature deficiency disorder........93
New Deal..................................75
Ode to a Child........................101

plugged-in..........................47, 103
plutocracy...............16, 18, 75, 76
political rhetoric........................16
poverty......60, 83, 91, 92, 99, 100
power elite.....................24, 28, 42
pre-determinism............43, 44, 46
prison system..................100, 121
proletariat............................49, 50
Protestant ethos......44, 46, 80, 87, 91, 94, 133
Protestant work-ethic................39
Protestantism...24, 37, 38, 41, 43, 44, 46, 47
re-creation.........................94, 120
Reaganomics.............................76
Reformation...................37, 42, 80
reframing.....................87, 94, 119
Roosevelt, Franklin...................75
sacred vs secular.....77-81, 83, 91, 133
schizophrenia.......6, 9, 11, 17, 81, 83, 94, 117
schizophrenic.....8, 13, 17, 20, 54, 85
secondhand desire...........104, 105
self image....................................4
Shaw, George Bernard............110
shopaholics...............................89
Smith, Adam...............77, 78, 133
Social Darwinism.........16, 55-63, 70, 133
Social Spiritualism classes.....104, 105, 114, 117-120

136

INDEX

Socrates 15
Spencer, Herbert 56, 57, 133
Spiritual Unification 125, 133
split personality 6
split social self 5, 6
survival of the fittest 56, 63
Tables
    Cultural *I* vs Cultural *ME* 16
    Industrialization
        vs Globalization 70
    Sacred vs Secular 79

The Corporation 17, 18
unfit 56, 59-61
unregulated capitalism 70, 71
WASP 24, 26, 27
Weber models
    Protestant Ethos 43
    Social Darwinism 58
    Spiritual Unification 125
Weber, Max ... 41-45, 58, 125, 133
Welfare Capitalism 50, 51, 82
zeitgeist 28, 115, 116

www.ingramcontent.com/pod-product-compliance
Lightning Source LLC
Chambersburg PA
CBHW021440080526
44588CB00009B/614